Essential Ketogenic Mediterranean Diet Cookbook

ESSENTIAL Ketogenic Mediterranean Diet Cookbook

100 Low-Carb, Heart-Healthy Recipes for Lasting Weight Loss

Molly Devine, RD

PHOTOGRAPHY BY EVI ABELER

callisto
publishing
an imprint of Sourcebooks

Published by Callisto Publishing LLC C/O Sourcebooks LLC
P.O. Box 4410, Naperville, Illinois 60567-4410
(630) 961-3900
callistopublishing.com
Printed and Bound In China
OGP 14

For my family and friends
who turn food into an experience.

Contents

Introduction

First and foremost, I am a lover of all things food! My career as a health and nutrition professional really got its start long before my years of biology and human metabolism classes, clinical experience, and patient counseling. As a teenager, my best friend Erica and I used to pore through our parents' cookbooks and latest editions of *Bon Appétit* magazine and plan out elaborate eight-course meals for our families, complete with our siblings as our waitstaff. As a linguistics and Spanish major in college, I spent my junior year living with a host family in Madrid, Spain. My bedroom (closet, really) was off the kitchen, and I became fast friends with our family's cook, Muñi. Accompanying her one morning to procure the various ingredients for that afternoon's meal, I quickly learned why Mediterranean food tastes so darn good: Ingredients are bought fresh, in season, and prepared with love. Grocery shopping became a new art form, and with each local shop having a specialty (meat and poultry from the *carnicería*, bread from the *panadería*), quality of ingredients was a top priority. I adopted this same principle years later when I ran my personal chef and catering business, focusing on fresh, local, and sustainable ingredients for my customized healthy, family-style meals. Along the way, I discovered that I could blend my love of food and nutrition with my desire to help people achieve their health goals and I went back to school to obtain a dietetics degree.

Today, as a licensed and registered dietitian who specializes in integrative and functional nutrition, I take great pride in showing my patients that food truly is the best medicine we have available. Plain and simple, we are what we eat! I have spent the majority of my dietetic career focusing on the use of therapeutic ketogenic diets to help my patients achieve their best health, whether that means the reversal or prevention of chronic diseases such as type 2 diabetes, improved neurological function, hormone balance and fertility, management of depression and anxiety, improved gut health, or healthy weight maintenance. Through clinical practice and both patient and personal success, I am a firm believer that a well-formulated ketogenic diet is not only beneficial for many, but it's sustainable in the long term for lasting benefits and improved quality of life.

As with any nutrition therapy, it is important to emphasize quality and balance in the foods included, as well as to avoid those that can cause damage or prevent sustainability of practice. More recently, keto frenzy has taken over in many media outlets. On the one hand, I am grateful to see this incredibly beneficial nutrition therapy gain more acceptance in both the medical and wellness communities. However, some negative effects come with its widespread popularity as well. "Dirty Keto" is the name given by industry professionals to the imbalanced, often highly processed, and potentially very unhealthy versions of this otherwise promising way of eating. Unfortunately, the promise of a quick fix through a ketogenic diet has untrained bloggers and social media influencers capitalizing on the popularity of this diet trend and leading individuals down a very unhealthy path. A well-formulated ketogenic diet for health doesn't mean just taking the bun off your fast-food hamburger, substituting artificial sweetener in your favorite dessert recipe, or avoiding all vegetables for fear of carbohydrates. Rather, we need to include a wide variety of foods, including colorful vegetables, healthy proteins, plant-based fats, and (gasp) fruits in moderation. We need to blend the principles of the heart-healthy Mediterranean Diet with the proven benefits of a high-fat/low-carb meal plan to truly create the best medicine not found in any pill bottle: the Ketogenic Mediterranean Diet.

I believe in the importance of dietary education and want to empower you with the knowledge you need for long-term success and sustainability. In the first chapter of this book, I will lay out for you not just the *what* but the *why* behind the Ketogenic Mediterranean Diet, along with everything you need to know about what to expect from your body as it transitions to a new way of eating. Each of the 100 delicious recipes and meal plans that follow not only fit the ideal macronutrient profile for success but are designed for balance, taste, variety, and health. I hope you enjoy this way of eating as much as I do and have a little fun in the kitchen while you're at it!

CHAPTER ONE

The Ketogenic Mediterranean Diet Primer

Welcome to the Ketogenic Mediterranean Diet! Congratulations on taking such an important step toward improving your health and well-being through nutrition. I hope you enjoy this experience as much as my patients and I have. Understanding your body's needs and functions will help you feel more connected to the process and provide motivation to continue toward your goals. This chapter will explore the individual components of both a ketogenic and Mediterranean way of eating and explain how the two can be combined into one effective and sustainable diet. Once you've read the information in this chapter, you will have an understanding of not only what you will be eating but why you will be eating this way and how it will positively impact the way you feel inside and out. Let's dive in!

The Mediterranean Way

Before it was hailed as the best diet of 2019 by *U.S. News & World Report*, the Mediterranean Diet was recommended by health professionals for its many benefits. The correlation between lifestyle and heart health in Italy and Greece was noted first in the 1950s by American scientist Ancel Keys of the University of Minnesota School of Public Health. He later went on to publish the "Seven Countries Study," which examined the diets and lifestyles of people in seven Mediterranean countries who consumed high amounts of olive oil, fish, fiber, and antioxidant-rich vegetables and fruits and low levels of saturated fats. In these groups he found decreased levels of cardiovascular disease.

Since that time, many studies and clinical trials have shown that a Mediterranean Diet, characterized by a high intake of plant-based foods (vegetables, fruits, nuts, whole grains, and legumes) and olive oil; a moderate intake of fish and poultry; and a low intake of dairy products, red meat, and sweets reduces abdominal circumference, lowers "bad" LDL cholesterol, elevates "good" HDL cholesterol, lowers triglycerides, lowers blood pressure, and lowers the concentration of glucose in the blood.

So much of what I will discuss in this chapter relates to food and nutrition, but it is important to remember that the Mediterranean way is so much more than diet alone. Nutrition is key, but other lifestyle factors—such as physical activity, sleep, and emotional well-being—contribute to our health as well and cannot be forgotten. The culture of the Mediterranean countries that were initially studied focused on family, mindfulness around food preparation and enjoyment, active lifestyles, and a slower pace of life. Fast-paced life is a global epidemic in the twenty-first century, but many of these cultures continue to preserve these traditions. Meals are savored with loved ones. Walking is a key mode of transportation. Vacations are taken and enjoyed. One of my favorite quotes from a Spaniard: "In America, you live to work. In Spain, we work to live."

The Limits of the Mediterranean Diet

The Mediterranean Diet is by far one of the healthiest ways of eating. However, for some individuals looking for long-term and sustainable weight loss, blood sugar regulation, and hormonal balance, the Mediterranean Diet alone may not allow them to fully reach these goals. If you have insulin resistance, frequent intake of even "healthy" carbohydrate-dense foods—such as higher-sugar fruits, whole grains, and legumes—can lead to a plateau in weight loss, elevation in fasting blood glucose, and an increased desire for sweets and processed foods, making adherence to a traditional Mediterranean Diet harder long-term. Why? Carbohydrate-dense foods are digested more rapidly than proteins or fats, making them less satiating and portion control more difficult to regulate. We don't binge on pure fats like olive oil or butter, but on pure carbs such as bread and pasta. For many, eating the high levels of carbohydrates found in the traditional Mediterranean Diet can be a hinderance to achieving their health goals.

Why Add Keto?

A ketogenic diet is one that derives the majority of its calories from dietary fat, contains only moderate levels of protein, and is very low in carbohydrates. This forces the body to go into a "fat burn" mode, relying on both dietary fat sources and stored body fat for daily fuel. The result is healthy weight management, blood sugar regulation, and improvements in many other health markers, such as blood pressure and cholesterol.

The Mediterranean Diet has been well studied for decades and is shown to have a positive impact on the health of those who follow it. While ketogenic dietary intervention is a relatively new science, I believe that the principles of a low-carb/high-fat approach to health, combined with the Mediterranean Diet's focus on heart-healthy fats and colorful, low-sugar plant foods, will become the gold standard among many healthcare providers working with individuals battling obesity, diabetes, and other chronic diseases.

The Ketogenic Mediterranean Diet Explained

This brings us to the Ketogenic Mediterranean Diet—a diet that combines the high-fat, moderate-protein, and low-carb ratios of the keto diet with the heart-healthy and fiber-rich foods and healthy behaviors of the Mediterranean Diet and lifestyle. The best of both worlds, the Ketogenic Mediterranean Diet provides a whole host of health benefits, including:

Weight loss. This typically is more rapid when beginning the diet and tends to slow a bit after the first few weeks. When your body enters ketosis, it is able to utilize stored body fat for energy, which supports continued weight loss. Additionally, a fat-burning ketogenic state naturally suppresses appetite and cravings, making it very sustainable.

Long-term cardiac health. Contrary to the "old science" that saturated fat alone leads to heart disease, we are now learning that it is the combination of refined and processed carbohydrates and sugars with saturated fat that elevates risk for cardiovascular disease. By increasing the consumption of unsaturated fats, as well as lowering the consumption of carbohydrates and sugars, the Ketogenic Mediterranean Diet and lifestyle can improve "good" cholesterol (HDL) and lower "bad" cholesterol (LDL), which is associated with a lower risk for cardiovascular disease. We also see a decrease in blood triglycerides (fat molecules in the blood) and the concentration of small particle size LDL cholesterol, both of which, when elevated, are key risk factors for heart disease.

Diabetes management. Studies show a ketogenic diet can reduce blood sugar and insulin fluctuations, due to reduced carbohydrate consumption. Better insulin control and reducing insulin resistance can help improve the associated metabolic disorders, as well as symptoms linked to high insulin and blood sugar, such as type 2 diabetes.

Sex hormone regulation. Women who suffer from polycystic ovary syndrome (PCOS) and related infertility may find relief with this way of eating. By avoiding insulin spikes while following a ketogenic lifestyle, women with PCOS report a reversal of increased androgen hormones, specifically testosterone, which leads to a reduction in their symptoms and increased fertility.

Thyroid health and longevity. Along with balancing sex hormones, a ketogenic lifestyle has a positive effect on thyroid hormones as well. A very low-carb diet tends to drive down T3, the main active thyroid hormone. A ketogenic lifestyle is positively correlated with improved thyroid health and overall longevity.

Improved cognitive function, energy, and mood. Eating a high-fat, low-carb diet provides steady energy without the crashes that are associated with eating a high-carb diet. When the body is in ketosis, the brain utilizes ketones, a more efficient fuel source than glucose, which leads to feeling more alert and mentally energized throughout the day. The ketogenic diet is currently being studied for its potential beneficial impacts on other neurological diseases, such as Alzheimer's and Parkinson's disease.

Better gut health. Many individuals suffering from irritable bowel syndrome (IBS) symptoms have found relief with a high-fat/low-carb way of eating. Many of the "bad" bacteria in our gut that create bloating, gas, and other GI complications live off a steady stream of glucose from carbohydrate-rich foods. When their food source is limited, they die off, leading to a healthier balance of "good" and "bad" bacteria, improved digestion and immunity, and reduced inflammation. Contrary to the belief that too little fiber intake from few dietary carbohydrates will lead to poor gut health, studies show that the human gut microbiota can actually utilize dietary fats to sustain growth and healthy gut function.

KETOGENIC DIET

High-fat dairy and eggs

Saturated fats from animal products, coconut oil, and MCT oil

High-fat meats and poultry

Moderate protein and very low carbohydrate

No added sugars

KETOGENIC MEDITERRANEAN DIET

Heart-healthy unsaturated fats

Quality proteins, including fatty fish

Colorful non-starchy vegetables and low-sugar fruits

Nuts and seeds

Whole-foods based

No processed foods, refined carbohydrates, and sugars

Moderate red wine

Adequate hydration

Healthy lifestyle

MEDITERRANEAN DIET

Limited dairy and eggs

Limited saturated fats

Unlimited carbs from whole grains, fruits and starchy vegetables

Unlimited legumes

Unlimited lean proteins

No regulation of portion size

Limited natural sweeteners

Getting to Ketogenic Mediterranean

Understanding Macros and Ratios on the Ketogenic Mediterranean Diet

Macronutrients—or "macros," for short—are the building blocks of our diet. All food breaks down into one of three macronutrients: protein, carbohydrates, or fat. Many foods, such as dairy or nuts, are a combination of two or all three. The generally recommended macro ratio for a standard ketogenic diet is 70 to 75 percent fat, 20 to 25 percent protein, and 5 to 10 percent carbohydrates. This means that 70 to 75 percent of your overall daily energy (in the form of calories) comes from fat, 20 to 25 percent comes from protein, and only 5 to 10 percent comes from carbohydrates. However, everyone's body is different and certain individuals have higher protein needs and/or can tolerate higher levels of carbohydrates from high-fiber, plant-based sources while remaining ketogenic.

Why do macros matter? Our bodies have a hierarchy of how they burn fuel, and fat is the last to go. If glucose (from carbohydrates), glycogen (the form of glucose the body stores for short-term use), or another energy source (such as amino acids from protein) is available, our bodies will use that as a fuel source before burning fat. One of the biggest differences between a ketogenic diet and simply a low-carb/high-protein diet is the moderation of protein. That's because our bodies can turn excess protein (and, in small amounts, excess fat) into glucose for use as fuel before turning to dietary or stored fat. This process is called *gluconeogenesis* and is a normal daily process, even for those on a ketogenic diet, because glucose is essential for a small number of cells and body functions. However, when dietary protein is in excess of what the body needs on a regular basis, the body will continue to run on glucose, preventing it from burning fat. Most people overconsume protein, thinking that it only goes to their muscles and makes them stronger. In fact, most people cannot absorb more than 25 to 35 grams of protein per meal, equal to about 4 to 6 ounces of meat or fish.

I recommend adhering to the standard macro ratio and limiting carbohydrates to under 35 grams per day for the initial two to four weeks of the Ketogenic Mediterranean Diet (Phase 1) to promote a faster and more effective transition to ketosis. Then you can, if your body tolerates it, raise your carbohydrate intake, through an increase in fiber-rich non-starchy vegetables, low-sugar fruits and nuts, up to 50 grams per day (Phase 2). All of the recipes in this book are appropriate for Phase 1. The majority of the carbohydrates in these recipes come from nutrient-rich non-starchy vegetables which are vital to overall health. Following the Mediterranean Diet principles of including a variety of colorful plant-based foods, some of the recipes will be higher in fiber and nutrient-rich carbohydrates than the standard ketogenic macro ratios which often don't include adequate vitamins and minerals. However, it is important to think about your overall macro intake across the day to put a slightly higher carbohydrate meal into perspective.

There are many online resources that can be useful for calculating your individual macronutrient needs based on your age, height, weight, and activity level. If you would like to have specific daily targets, I suggest using an app such as MyFitnessPal or Cronometer, both of which have free versions. The meal plans and recipes that follow are designed around a 1,400 to 1,500 daily calorie goal, which for most people will result in weight loss without having to calculate macros or track foods. To adjust this up or down, you can change the serving size of each recipe based on hunger, progress, and individual lifestyle needs.

A Word on Fats

The Ketogenic Mediterranean Diet is chock-full of excellent sources of heart-healthy and anti-inflammatory omega-3 fatty acids, such as fatty fish, eggs, nuts, and seeds. Animal products are also great sources of omega-3 fatty acids but quality is so important. When animals are fed a grain-based feed containing soy and corn, this elevates their ratio of omega-6 fatty acids. That's why you should aim for grass-fed meats and dairy; pasture-raised or free-range poultry, pork, and eggs; and wild-caught seafood, whenever possible. Use mostly olive oil and grass-fed butter (in moderation) when cooking and avoid processed cooking oils, such as canola, corn, and soy. Look out for these oils, which are common in condiments such as mayonnaise and bottled salad dressings. Choose instead to make your own versions with the recipes provided in this book. Avoiding processed and "boxed" foods will largely reduce your omega-6 fatty acid consumption and help promote an anti-inflammatory and healthy lifestyle.

Achieving Ketosis and Becoming Keto-Adapted

When following a ketogenic diet, you are more than changing what you eat—you are changing how your body processes food and creates energy. Most people are glucose-burners. This means they use glucose, mainly from carbohydrates, as their main fuel source to carry out everyday function and activity. Unfortunately, due to a more sedentary lifestyle, most people consume more glucose than they need for activity, causing them to also become glucose-savers. Excess glucose gets stored in the body, either as glycogen or adipose tissue (fat cells), which are much harder to get rid of.

Think of glycogen as your bank savings account: You'd really rather use your checking account (circulating glucose), but you'll dip into this savings account to pay your bills if you really need to. However, once glucose is converted and stored in fat cells, your body views it more like your 401(k) or retirement fund. You're not going to spend that unless absolutely necessary and no other funds are available.

The ketogenic diet is a way of eating that switches the body from being a glucose-burner to a fat-burner, utilizing both dietary fat from meals as well as stored body fat outside of mealtimes to produce a new fuel called a *ketone* for its main energy source. This natural fat-burning metabolic state is called *ketosis*, which is where the ketogenic diet gets its name.

When you first begin this way of eating and drastically reduce your carbohydrate intake, your body will continue to look for glucose for energy. Most people have two to three days' worth of glycogen (stored glucose) and will begin the process of breaking down this storage for energy within the first day. Each molecule of glycogen is one glucose molecule with water molecules attached to it. As we liberate the glucose to send to our cells for energy, we release all this stored water along with it. Water weight loss is great and will help reduce joint stiffness, bloating, and produce a result on the scale.

Once your body has depleted most of its glycogen storage—we never fully get rid of it, because our body needs glucose for some functions and is protective of this—it will need to look for a new fuel source to power the body and brain. We'll make an abundance of dietary fatty acids and stored body fat available to the body for use but not all cells can use pure fatty acids for fuel and, most importantly, the brain cannot use them at all.

Ketosis is the body's process of converting these fatty acids into usable currency for energy: a ketone. Fatty acids travel to the liver, are converted into ketones, and sent throughout the body and to the brain for use as energy. Ketones are like the rocket fuel of gas: They are extremely efficient, provide long-term energy, and improve function. However, they are expensive for the body to make and require a lot more energy input than glucose. As soon as the body has a new source for glucose from the ingestion of carbohydrates or from excess protein, it will halt ketone production and go right back to the cheap gas. Along with that comes the return of hunger, cravings, brain fog, water retention, and dips in energy.

Once your body has entered ketosis and starts to become more and more efficient at the production and use of ketones as its primary fuel source, you can expect a reduction in hunger, improvement in energy, increased mental clarity, improved sleep, and reduction in inflammation. I believe these are the best indicators of a true state of ketosis, but for those who want to measure their progress and ketone production in a more "clinical" way, you can do so using either blood ketone meters, breath ketone meters, or urine sticks.

"Keto Flu"

The quick dumping of stored fluid as the body breaks down stored glycogen within the first few days of starting a ketogenic diet can lead to dehydration from a loss of electrolytes along with the water. Many people talk about experiencing a "keto flu" when trying a ketogenic diet for the first time; however, symptoms of "keto flu" are the same as clinical dehydration and can easily be avoided with these tips:

Stay hydrated! As a general rule, I suggest half of your body weight in ounces, so if you weigh 200 pounds, aim for 100 ounces of water a day. This can come in the form of unsweetened teas, seltzers, or fruit-infused waters.

Keep up with your electrolytes. The main four are sodium, potassium, calcium, and magnesium. Avocados are high in potassium and magnesium. Nuts, seeds, and fatty fish such as salmon and mackerel are good sources of magnesium. You can also drink some chicken or beef broth, which is high in sodium, to boost electrolytes. However, if you are on a medically supervised low-sodium diet, consult with your doctor before increasing sodium levels.

Attack carb cravings with fat! You are trying to retrain your cells and brain to look for fat as a primary fuel source rather than glucose from carbs. By giving it fat when a craving for sugars or carbs hits, you are reinforcing this process and encouraging your body to make the transition.

The Challenges of the Ketogenic Mediterranean Diet

Nutrition and lifestyle change can be hard and I understand that. In this section, I want to address some potential concerns and challenges of adopting the Ketogenic Mediterranean Diet and provide you with the support you need to find success in this lifestyle.

The biggest change in adopting a ketogenic approach will be the reduction in carbohydrates from grains, higher-sugar fruits, and starchy vegetables. A sustainable lifestyle does not mean you will never eat your favorite fruits or starchy vegetables again but remember that a key first goal to the success of this way of eating is to shift your metabolic pathway from being glucose-burning to fat-burning. It is important to follow the ratios outlined in the next section closely to promote that transition.

If you worry your sweet tooth or pasta addiction will be difficult to overcome, it is important to understand the transition that happens within the brain as the body makes this metabolic shift. When the brain is running on glucose as its primary fuel source, it craves the richest sources of this energy regularly: sweets, breads, pasta, rice, and other carb-heavy foods. However, when the body is in ketosis, the brain is fueled by ketones rather than glucose, receiving a steady stream of these energy powerhouses from the breakdown of fatty acids by the liver. Cravings for glucose-rich carbohydrates diminish significantly, satiety from nutrient-dense healthy fats and quality proteins prevents hunger, and the constant desire for carbohydrate-rich foods goes away.

For those currently following a ketogenic diet higher in saturated fat and lower in nutrient-rich vegetables and unsaturated fats, you may have concern over missing some of your regular keto staples, such as heavy whipping cream, coconut oil, and bacon. As I have noted previously in this chapter, saturated fat does not have to be avoided entirely. The Ketogenic Mediterranean Diet places an emphasis on increasing heart-healthy unsaturated fats while including saturated fats in moderation to provide the best possible health outcomes and sustainability. Again, combining the healthiest principles of each of these separate dietary interventions leads to a new, truly sustainable and superpowered way of eating. The tasty recipes and detailed meal plans in this book will quickly make you a happy convert!

Your Ketogenic Mediterranean Kitchen

As with any way of eating, a well-stocked kitchen can make meal preparation and sticking to the diet so much easier. The following list is a great starting point to load up your kitchen with some basics for quick meals, snacks, and many of the staple ingredients found in the recipes that follow.

Pantry Essentials

- Artichoke hearts

- Broth or stock: chicken, beef, or vegetable

- Canned seafood: salmon, sardines, anchovies, mackerel, herring, clams, and low-mercury tuna

- Nut and seed butters: almond, sunflower, and tahini (no sugar added)

- Nuts: almonds, walnuts, pecans, macadamia nuts, hazelnuts, Brazil nuts, and pistachios

- Oils: olive oil and avocado oil

- Seeds: flaxseed, chia seeds, pumpkin seeds, and sesame seeds

- Seltzer waters (unsweetened, artificially or naturally)

- Spices: cinnamon, allspice, pumpkin pie spice (no sugar added), ground ginger, cumin, chili powder, garlic powder, onion powder, and a curry blend

- Teas: herbal, black, and green (no sugar added)

- Tomatoes: canned, diced, and puréed (no sugar added) tomatoes and sun-dried tomatoes

- Vinegars: apple cider vinegar and red wine vinegar

Refrigerated and Frozen Essentials

- Butter, grass-fed

- Capers

- Cheeses: mozzarella, Parmesan, goat cheese, Manchego (Spanish sheep's milk cheese), and feta (preferably sheep's milk)

- Eggs (preferably free-range)

- Fresh and frozen vegetables: broccoli, dark leafy greens, green beans, asparagus, Brussels sprouts, bell peppers, cauliflower, riced cauliflower, green and yellow squash, cucumber, cherry tomatoes, jicama, radishes, snow peas, and carrots (avoid frozen vegetable blends containing peas, corn, beans, and potatoes)

- Frozen berries: strawberries, blueberries, raspberries, and blackberries

- Olives

- Pesto (look for those made with olive oil)

- Salad greens: arugula, spinach, kale, baby lettuces, romaine, and endive

Other Perishables

- Avocados

- Citrus: lime, lemon, and clementine

- Fresh herbs: basil, rosemary, parsley, and thyme

- Fresh tomatoes

- Garlic

- Onions: red, yellow, or white

"Nice to Have" Ingredients

These ingredients are not imperative to a healthy and well-stocked Ketogenic Mediterranean kitchen. Most of these are found in "sweet treats" recipes, so feel free to avoid them if you prefer more savory foods.

- Almond flour or almond meal, for baking

- Medium-chain triglyceride (MCT) oil: While technically a saturated fat, the unique length of this fatty acid allows it to be absorbed differently in our digestive tract, allowing for immediate conversion to ketones rather than storage in fat cells.

- Natural, sugar-free sweeteners: stevia, liquid stevia, Truvia, monk fruit extract, and erythritol

- Unsweetened cocoa powder

A Note on Sweeteners

When asking anyone to eliminate sugar from their diet, I am constantly asked about sugar substitutes. Sure, they are a better alternative to the hard stuff because they won't cause blood sugar or insulin spikes, but they are like putting a Band-Aid on a gunshot wound.

Here's why: Non-nutritive sweeteners (Splenda, stevia, Truvia, Equal) are 200 to 700 times sweeter than their "natural" counterpart. When we use these substitutes, we don't train our taste buds to adapt to a less-sweet product, but rather tell them to crave even sweeter foods, making breaking the sugar addiction that much more difficult.

What about sugar alcohols, such as erythritol? While not as super-sweet as non-nutritive sweeteners, they do still produce a small effect on blood sugar levels and insulin response, which we want to avoid on a ketogenic diet. Another downside is that they can cause bloating and diarrhea when consumed in excess, especially in individuals predisposed to food sensitivities and gut imbalance.

Recently, monk fruit extract has gained popularity as a "healthier" alternative. While this may be the best option for gut health and avoidance of other negative side effects, I still caution the use of excess sweeteners of any kind in your diet.

Bottom line: Sugar substitutes are okay to use in dessert recipes when you have a hankering for something sweet, but these foods should still be thought of as "treats" and not staples in your day-to-day diet. Moderation is the name of the game! In chapter 9, I provide recipes that help you learn to use other flavoring agents like fruit and spices to create "sweet treats" without compromising your progress and adaptation to the Ketogenic Mediterranean lifestyle. As you become fully keto-adapted, your body naturally reduces cravings for carbohydrates and sugars, so listen to your body and help your taste buds adapt with the rest of the new you.

Foods to Enjoy and Avoid

	ENJOY	IN MODERATION	AVOID
VEGETABLES	Leafy greens, green beans, asparagus, cruciferous vegetables, zucchini, yellow squash, bell peppers, celery, mushrooms, eggplant, pickles, garlic, radishes	Carrots, pumpkin and other winter squash, onions, tomatoes	Potatoes, yams, corn, peas
FISH AND SEAFOOD	High-fat, lower-mercury fish, such as wild-caught salmon, mackerel, herring, sardines, and anchovies; shellfish		
MEATS AND PROTEINS	Grass-fed beef and lamb, pasture-raised pork, free-range poultry, free-range eggs	Bacon; cured meats, like prosciutto and salami	Processed meats, like Spam, hot dogs, and deli meat
DAIRY AND CHEESE	Full-fat cheese, especially those prevalent in the Mediterranean, whole-milk Greek yogurt	Grass-fed butter, heavy cream, sour cream, cream cheese	Sweetened yogurts, milk, low-fat or part-skim cheeses
GRAINS AND LEGUMES		Peanuts	All others
FRUITS	Avocados, berries, lemons, limes	Oranges and clementines	High-sugar fruits (e.g., apples, pears, peaches, plums, cherries, melons, bananas, and other tropical fruits)

	ENJOY	IN MODERATION	AVOID
NUTS, SEEDS, AND FLOURS	All tree nuts and nut butters, chia and flax seeds; pumpkin seeds; sesame seeds and tahini	Almond flour, pistachios	White flour, whole-wheat flour, chickpea flour
FATS AND OILS	Olive oil; olives; avocado oil; avocado oil mayonnaise	MCT oil	Processed vegetable oils (e.g., canola, corn, and soybean oil)
SWEETENERS, SPICES, AND SEASONINGS	Herbs. unsweetened spices, vanilla extract; red wine vinegar; stone-ground mustard; unsweetened hot sauce; Worcestershire sauce	Balsamic vinegar, monk fruit, stevia, erythritol	Sugar of any kind (honey, maple syrup, brown sugar, cane sugar, corn syrup, and agave), ketchup, barbeque sauce, seasoning blends that include sugar (e.g. cinnamon-sugar blend)
BEVERAGES	Water, unsweetened flavored seltzer waters, unsweetened teas	Black coffee, red wine, fruit-infused waters, plant-based milks, unsweetened spirits	Sodas, juices, beer, cow's milk, sweetened teas and coffee drinks

Kitchen Equipment and Tools

These are the kitchen tools and equipment that make these delicious and fresh Ketogenic Mediterranean meals come together in a flash.

Must-Haves

Colander. A medium to large colander will serve a variety of uses.

Cutting boards. Wood, composite, and synthetic are all fine. I recommend a medium- to large-size board to maximize your work surface.

Dry and liquid measuring cups and spoons. Get these in a variety of sizes.

Glass or ceramic baking dishes (8-by-8-inch and 9-by-13-inch). These are a great alternative to roasting pans.

Proper knives. The most important tools for any chef. I recommend having a larger chef's knife, a smaller paring knife, and a serrated knife.

Roasting pans and/or baking sheets. There is no need to invest in expensive baking sheets—any will do.

Saucepans and skillets. To double any of the recipes, you will want to have larger pots and pans for cooking. I love using a 10- to 12-inch cast iron skillet, but a medium-size skillet will work too.

Whisk. A simple medium-size whisk will help make sauces smooth and eggs fluffy.

Nice-to-Haves

Dutch oven or oven-safe covered baking dish. Great for slow cooking meats for flavor and tenderness in the oven.

Food processor. This is a little more of an investment, but the monetary and time savings from homemade riced cauliflower, dressings, sauces, and nut butters will pay off. I recommend at least an 8-cup capacity.

Immersion blender. Great for making smoothies, dressings, sauces, and soups. You can purchase one for under $30.

Silicone ice cube trays. Use these for making homemade sweet or savory fat bombs. Stick to the standard ice cube size for easy portion control.

Spiralizer. Get creative with a variety of vegetables to create noodle-free versions of Mediterranean favorites. You can purchase a simple spiralizer for under $20.

Storage containers for fridge and freezer. Glass or BPA-free plastic is preferred.

Zester or box grater. I use the same tool for zesting citrus as I do for finely grating cheeses. Choosing a grater with a medium grate will allow for this versatility.

Putting the "Lifestyle" in Lifestyle Diet

The following lifestyle habits may not be changes for you but should be included regularly while adapting to the Ketogenic Mediterranean Diet. I always recommend small steps when implementing any sort of lifestyle or behavior change. When we set the bar too high, we often give up early on. Focus on the routine rather than the duration.

Practice good sleep hygiene. Stick to a regular bedtime and waketime routine, regardless of the day. Avoid all electronics 30 minutes prior to bedtime. Aim to have your last meal of the day at least 1 hour before bedtime to avoid digestive discomfort. Set a goal of 6 to 8 hours of sleep nightly.

Set aside time for yourself daily. Whether through exercise, meditation, reading, journaling, listening to music, or a relaxing bath, it is important to help your body handle everyday stress.

Incorporate physical activity catered to your abilities and preferences. If you hate the gym, don't force yourself to go; it will only add stress. Walking with a friend (or solo), biking, swimming, dancing, and stretching are all wonderful ways to relieve stress and reduce inflammation. Set a goal of some sort of movement daily.

Avoid mealtime distractions. Turn off the TV, put down the phone, don't eat lunch while working at your desk, and avoid eating in the car. Making a point to focus on the delicious meal in front of you will help you gain a better understanding of your own satiety and your body's needs.

Eat at a table. Light a candle, add fresh flowers, and make your environment pleasing. You'll be amazed at how this can elevate even the most common meals.

Enjoy meals with friends and family. If you have a family with busy schedules, set a goal of having at least two meals together a week. If you are cooking for one, invite friends over once a week and enjoy a new recipe together.

Adhere to a regular meal routine. Life is busy and this is sometimes hard to do, but generally sticking to regular mealtimes will help your body regulate hunger, blood sugar control, and optimize digestion.

Tips to Set Yourself Up for Success

Changing dietary habits can be hard. The tips in this section will help you successfully start the Ketogenic Mediterranean Diet and move toward a lifelong journey of better health:

Don't go hungry. Even if your primary goal is weight loss, the Ketogenic Mediterranean Diet does not rely on caloric restriction for success but rather focuses on the types and quality of the foods in your meals. Cravings will lessen and natural satiety will dominate as your body adjusts but, in the first few weeks, don't worry about how many snacks you may need to include during the day, as long as they are Ketogenic Mediterranean Diet friendly.

Attack carb or sugar cravings with fat. Remember that you're retraining your brain from searching for glucose for energy to learning to utilize ketones, so if you have a carb craving, attack it with a "fatty" snack instead. Have convenient "fatty" snacks on hand at work or in your bag so you're not caught off guard.

Create new routines. Replace your old unhealthy routines with something new. Make a mug of herbal tea after dinner instead of having dessert, eat meals at a table and free of distractions, or take a 5- to 10-minute walk to decompress at the end of your day.

Strength in numbers. Share your goals with the important people in your life. Organize group meal prep days, have a friend over for dinner, or set up weekly phone check-ins with an old friend. Surrounding yourself with a great support network can help you get through difficult days, as well as provide encouragement and celebration for your accomplishments.

Be kind to yourself. Rome was not built in a day. You may have cravings or symptoms of sugar withdrawal, such as headaches or irritability. Make sure to give your body what it needs to be successful. Get adequate sleep, and don't overdo it with exercise—you may need to cut back on your current physical activity until your body has adjusted. Understand that everybody's rate of success is different and you can't compare yourself to others.

Don't weigh yourself every day. There are many reasons why the scale may go up or down for no apparent reason and weighing yourself daily often leads to frustration. Move to weekly weigh-ins or pick a different measure for success entirely, such as improvements in body composition, increased energy levels, better mood, and lowered fasting blood glucose.

Decline the wine . . . at least at first. The Ketogenic Mediterranean Diet allows for the occasional glass of red wine once the body is in ketosis, but alcohol can hinder this progress initially. Even though dry red wine is low in carbs and sugar, it must be processed by the liver for detoxification and will be the first calories used for energy, ahead of fat, protein, or carbohydrates. Remember that the liver is also in charge of converting fatty acids to ketones for energy, so if it is busy detoxifying, it won't be very effective at making ketones and energy production and weight loss will be slowed.

Think of saturated fats as a guest star, not the main attraction. Red meat, fattier cured meats like bacon and prosciutto, butter, and cheeses shouldn't be the main part of your meal, but they lend a great flavor to many traditional Mediterranean dishes. Fortunately, a little can go a long way. Crumble a slice of bacon or slice a couple ounces of steak on top of a vibrant leafy salad with a flavorful vinaigrette for an easy lunch or dinner. A couple times a month, though, you can let the guest star take center stage.

Plan ahead. The best way to turn diet intention into diet reality is to plan and prep meals ahead of time. The meal plans and recipes in the following chapters are intended to provide you with a clear path to success for the next two transition weeks. Make sure to have convenient snacks on hand, pack your lunch, and have dinner ingredients prepped or meals already prepared, so there are no excuses to abandon your good intentions at the end of a busy day.

CHAPTER TWO

14-Day Meal Plan and Beyond

Now it's time to get started! I have designed a two-week meal plan to fit the ideal macronutrient ratios for a successful transition into ketosis using the wide variety of delicious recipes found in this book. However, feel free to adjust the amount of cooking to fit your needs and preferences. Some people need a lot of variety in their meals and don't enjoy eating the same thing twice. Others tend to thrive on routine and, once they find a breakfast or lunch that works, they don't mind having that every day to keep things simple. Do whatever works best for you.

◀ Garlicky Shrimp with Mushrooms, page 108,
Taste of the Mediterranean Fat Bombs, page 67,
Harissa Oil, page 173

About the Meal Plans

Many recipes can be made in advance to free up your time during the week, and some meals will have leftovers that will be eaten again during the week (or in the following week). When this is the case, those meals are marked with an asterisk in the meal plans. You'll find a shopping list for each week with all the fresh ingredients you'll need. If you decide to double up recipes and omit others, you will need to modify these shopping lists. The pantry and canned goods section under Week 1 will be used throughout the two weeks, so stock up on these items before beginning and buy the fresh ingredients weekly.

Snack options are included, but they are there only if you feel hungry between meals. The ingredients for the snacks are not included on the shopping lists, so be sure to add them if you plan on making them. Snacks are helpful during the first week, when your body has not fully transitioned into ketosis. However, as your body adjusts, you will likely begin to feel more satiety and less need for snacking, which is a great sign your body is making a metabolic shift. Part of this process is learning to listen to your body, and if you don't feel the need for snacks, then by all means omit them.

The weekend plans include a "brunch" meal, a heavier afternoon "snack," and a "dinner." You can stick to the breakfast, lunch, and dinner schedule of the weekday, but pushing breakfast later may come naturally as you enter ketosis and feel more satiated from the higher-fat and filling meals.

	BREAKFAST / BRUNCH	LUNCH / AFTERNOON SNACK	DINNER
M	Mediterranean Frittata (page 39)	Avocado Gazpacho (page 73) and Manchego Crackers* (page 61)	Zucchini Lasagna* (page 93)
T	Morning Buzz Iced Coffee (page 38)	Orange-Tarragon Chicken Salad Wrap (page 78) with leftover Manchego Crackers (page 61)	Lamb Kofte with Yogurt Sauce (page 134) and Israeli Salad with Nuts and Seeds* (page 83)
W	Avocado Toast (page 44)	Leftover Zucchini Lasagna (page 93)	Swordfish in Tarragon-Citrus Butter* (page 109) with leftover Israeli Salad with Nuts and Seeds (page 83)
T	Green Goddess Smoothie (page 40)	Leftover Swordfish in Tarragon-Citrus Butter over spinach (page 109)	Lemon-Rosemary Spatchcock Chicken* (page 132) with spinach salad dressed in Simple Vinaigrette* (page 170)
F	Sweet 'n' Savory Toast with Burrata and Berries (page 50)	Leftover Lemon-Rosemary Spatchcock Chicken (page 132) over mixed greens	Rosemary-Lemon Snapper Baked in Parchment (page 119) Garlicky Broccoli Rabe with Artichokes* (page 87)
S	Egg Baked in Avocado (page 49) with Burrata Caprese Stack (page 62)	Zucchini-Ricotta Fritters with Lemon-Garlic Aioli (page 63) with Citrus-Marinated Olives (page 58)	Shrimp Ceviche Salad (page 114) (make Saturday morning) with leftover Manchego Crackers (page 61)
S	Crustless Greek Cheese Pie (page 51) and Morning Buzz Iced Coffee (page 38)	Smoked Salmon Crudités (page 57) with leftover Manchego Crackers (page 61)	Stuffed Pork Loin with Sun-Dried Tomato and Goat Cheese* (page 143) with leftover Garlicky Broccoli Rabe with Artichokes (page 87)

Week 1 Snack Ideas

- Manchego Crackers (page 61)
- Goat Cheese–Mackerel Pâté (page 66)
- Marzipan Fat Bomb (page 154)
- Almond butter and celery sticks

Week 1 Shopping List

PRODUCE

- Avocados (9)
- Baby arugula (4 cups)
- Baby spinach leaves or mixed greens (16 ounces)
- Basil, fresh (1 bunch)
- Bell peppers, red (2)
- Bibb lettuce (1 head)
- Broccoli rabe (2 pounds)
- Cherry tomatoes (1 pint)
- Cilantro, fresh (1 bunch)
- Clementines (6)
- Cucumbers, medium, preferably seedless (5)
- Endive spears or Bibb lettuce leaves (8)
- Garlic (3 or 4 heads)
- Lemons (9)
- Limes (8)
- Mint, fresh (1 bunch)
- Onions, red, small (2)
- Parsley, Italian flat-leaf, fresh (1 bunch)
- Rosemary, fresh (1 bunch)
- Scallions (1 bunch)
- Tarragon, fresh (1 bunch)
- Tomatoes, preferably heirloom (4)
- Zucchini, large (5)

SEAFOOD, POULTRY, AND MEAT

- Chicken thighs, boneless, skinless (or leftover rotisserie chicken) (2 to 3)

- Chicken, whole (1 [3- to 4-pound] roaster)

- Lamb or ground beef, preferably grass-fed (1 pound)

- Pork tenderloin (1½ pounds)

- Red snapper (1¼ pounds)

- Shrimp, preferably wild-caught (1 pound)

- Smoked wild salmon (6 ounces)

- Swordfish steaks (1 pound)

DAIRY/EGGS

- Burrata or mozzarella cheese, fresh (6 ounces)

- Butter, grass-fed (1 stick)

- Eggs, large, preferably free-range (13)

- Feta cheese (8 ounces)

- Goat cheese, soft (6 ounces)

- Greek yogurt, plain, whole-milk (32 ounces)

- Manchego or sheep's milk cheese (4 ounces)

- Mozzarella cheese, whole-milk (8 ounces)

- Parmesan cheese (5 ounces)

- Ricotta cheese, whole-milk (40 ounces)

FROZEN ITEMS

- Mixed frozen berries (½ cup)

- Spinach (1 [24-ounce] bag)

CANNED AND BOTTLED ITEMS

- Artichoke hearts (2 [13.75-ounce] cans)

- Capers (1 [3.5-ounce] jar)

- Marinara sauce, low-sugar (1 [24-ounce] jar)

- Olives, green, whole (2 [8-ounce] jars)

- Olives, Kalamata, pitted (1 [8-ounce] jar)

- Pesto (2 [8-ounce] jars)

- Red salmon (1 [14.5-ounce] can or 1 pound fresh)
- Tomatoes, crushed (1 [28-ounce] can)

- Tomatoes, sun-dried, oil-packed (1 [8-ounce] jar)
- White wine, dry (1 cup)
- Yellowfin tuna, olive oil-packed (4 [4-ounce] cans)

PANTRY ITEMS

- Allspice, ground
- Almond butter, unsweetened
- Almond extract
- Almonds, slivered
- Baking powder
- Baking soda
- Bay leaves
- Black pepper
- Breadcrumbs, panko
- Cinnamon, ground
- Coffee
- Cumin, ground
- Dill, dried
- Flaxseed
- Flour, almond
- Garlic powder
- Ginger, ground
- Harissa

- Mayonnaise, avocado oil
- Mustard, Dijon
- Nutmeg, ground
- Oil, extra-virgin olive
- Oregano, dried
- Paprika
- Pine nuts
- Pistachios, shelled
- Pumpkin seeds
- Red pepper flakes
- Salt
- Sunflower seeds, shelled
- Vanilla extract
- Vinegar, red wine
- Walnuts, halves or pieces

	BREAKFAST / BRUNCH	LUNCH / AFTERNOON SNACK	DINNER
M	Leftover Crustless Greek Cheese Pie (page 51; from Week 1)	Leftover Stuffed Pork Loin with Sun-Dried Tomato and Goat Cheese (page 143) with spinach salad dressed in leftover Simple Vinaigrette (page 170; from Week 1)	Salmon Cakes with Avocado* (page 123) and Roasted Eggplant with Mint and Harissa* (page 88)
T	Greek Yogurt Parfait (page 47)	Dilled Tuna Salad Sandwich* (page 75)	Meatballs in Creamy Almond Sauce* (page 136) with leftover Roasted Eggplant with Mint and Harissa (page 88)
W	Leftover Crustless Greek Cheese Pie (page 51; from Week 1)	Traditional Greek Salad* (page 76) with leftover Salmon Cakes with Avocado (page 123)	Leftover Meatballs in Creamy Almond Sauce (page 136) with salad greens dressed in leftover Simple Vinaigrette (page 170; from Week 1)
T	Blueberry Power Smoothie (page 41)	Leftover Traditional Greek Salad (page 76) with leftover Dilled Tuna Salad Sandwich (page 75)	Shrimp in Creamy Pesto over Zoodles* (page 120)
F	Baklava Hot Porridge (page 45)	Leftover Shrimp in Creamy Pesto over Zoodles (page 120) with salad greens dressed in leftover Simple Vinaigrette (page 170; from Week 1)	Shakshuka (page 89)
S	Lemon–Olive Oil Breakfast Cakes with Berry Syrup (page 46) and Greek Deviled Eggs (page 60)	Tuna Croquettes (page 55)	Flank Steak with Orange-Herb Pistou* (page 138) with salad greens dressed in leftover Simple Vinaigrette (page 170; from Week 1)
S	Florentine Breakfast Sandwich (page 43) and Morning Buzz Iced Coffee (page 38)	Salmon-Stuffed Cucumbers (page 65) and Marinated Feta and Artichokes (page 54)	Leftover Flank Steak with Orange-Herb Pistou (page 138) on Versatile Sandwich Round (page 169) with sliced tomato

Week 2 Snack Ideas

- Marinated Feta and Artichokes (page 54)
- Olive Tapenade with Anchovies (page 59)
- Nut Butter Cup Fat Bomb (page 153)
- ½ avocado with a drizzle of lime juice and a sprinkle of salt

Week 2 Shopping List

PRODUCE

- Avocados (4)
- Bell pepper, green (2)
- Bell pepper, red (1)
- Cauliflower, medium head (1)
- Cilantro, fresh (1 bunch)
- Cucumbers, seedless (4)
- Eggplant, medium (2)
- Garlic (3 to 4 heads)
- Lemons (4)
- Lime (1)
- Mint, fresh (1 bunch)
- Onions, red, small (3)
- Onions, yellow, small (3)
- Oranges (2)
- Oregano, fresh (1 bunch)
- Parsley, flat-leaf Italian, fresh (2 bunches)
- Scallions (1 bunch)
- Tomato, medium, preferably heirloom (1)
- Tomatoes, Roma (6)
- Zucchini, large (2)

SEAFOOD, POULTRY, MEAT

- Beef, ground, preferably grass-fed (8 ounces)

- Beef, flank steak, preferably grass-fed (1 pound)

- Shrimp, fresh, preferably wild-caught (1½ pounds)

- Veal or pork, ground (8 ounces)

DAIRY/EGGS

- Almond milk (1 [32-ounce] carton)

- Eggs, large, preferably free-range (2 dozen)

- Feta cheese (14 ounces)

- Goat cheese (4 ounces)

- Greek yogurt, plain, whole-milk (4 ounces)

- Heavy cream (1 pint)

- Mozzarella cheese, fresh (1 ounce)

FROZEN ITEMS

- Blueberries (¼ cup)

- Mixed berries (1¾ cups)

- Spinach (1 [6 to 8-ounce] bag)

Beyond the First 14 Days

I've said it before, and I'll say it again: Change is hard! Completing the initial stages of any new dietary routine is a huge accomplishment and you've made it! So, what's next? By now, you should be feeling more adjusted to this way of eating and have less hunger, fewer carb cravings, and, after an initial decrease, improved energy. These are all signs that your body is in ketosis. However, it may take longer for some than others, so do not despair if you haven't seen a huge change in the first two weeks. The following tips not only help deepen ketosis and maintain long-term success for those that have transitioned, but they can also help those who are struggling with the transition give their body a little nudge in the right direction.

Are you getting enough fat? In order for your body to become "keto-adapted," you must give it fat for it to learn how to use it as fuel. Don't be afraid of drizzling extra olive oil over that fish or salad—it will only help your body adapt to using fat for fuel.

Physical activity. After the first two weeks, you should be able to introduce more movement or go back to regular exercise routines. Moderate intensity, "fat burning" exercises such as walking, jogging, swimming, and biking are all great ways to help your body become more efficient at producing ketones for fuel. Higher intensity activities such as sprints or weightlifting will burn down glucose or glycogen more rapidly. High intensity interval training (HIIT) activities such as rounds of jumping jacks, sprints, or burpees can also help burn down glycogen stores faster if you are having trouble transitioning into ketosis.

Intermittent fasting. If weight loss is a goal of yours, your body must use its stored body fat, as well as dietary fat, as an energy source in between meals. One way to accomplish this is to shorten your "eating window" or practice intermittent fasting. The easiest way to do this is to push breakfast back later or drop it all together. The goal of this shift is not to decrease overall caloric intake, although that may happen naturally, but just to shorten the time in which you ingest that energy. Practicing intermittent fasting is like training for a marathon—it is a gradual progression. If dinner is typically at 7 p.m. and breakfast is at 7 a.m., you are on a 12/12 schedule (12 hours of eating and 12 hours of fasting). Try pushing breakfast back 30 minutes later every two to three days so that, in a few weeks, you can gradually go until 11 a.m. or noon before your first meal. You will have increased your "fasting window" to 16 to 17 hours, giving your body more time to work on burning stored body fat for more efficient ketone production as well as greater weight loss.

If you ever feel you have "fallen off the wagon" or just need a chance to reset, revisit the structured two-week meal plan at the beginning of this chapter to get yourself back on track. Remember, no one is perfect; moderation is the name of the game for long-term health and success in the Ketogenic Mediterranean lifestyle.

CHAPTER THREE

Breakfast, Brunch, and Smoothies

Morning Buzz Iced Coffee

EGG-FREE, GLUTEN-FREE, VEGETARIAN

Serves 1
Prep Time: 10 minutes

1 cup freshly brewed strong
  black coffee, cooled
  slightly
1 tablespoon extra-virgin
  olive oil
1 tablespoon half-and-half
  or heavy cream (optional)
1 teaspoon MCT oil
  (optional)
⅛ teaspoon almond extract
⅛ teaspoon ground
  cinnamon

A morning coffee dense with fats is the ketogenic alternative to a protein shake: It can serve as a quick and easy breakfast and keep you satiated for hours. Unfortunately, many versions contain nothing but saturated fats and don't fit into a Mediterranean Diet. For this version, use coffee made in a French press, a popular Mediterranean technique that results in a richer and more flavorful brew. Be sure to use quality coffee beans. I prefer organic, sustainably grown and roasted beans—the fresher, the better.

1. Pour the slightly cooled coffee into a blender or large glass (if using an immersion blender).

2. Add the olive oil, half-and-half (if using), MCT oil (if using), almond extract, and cinnamon.

3. Blend well until smooth and creamy. Drink warm and enjoy.

Per Serving: Calories: 128, Total Fat: 14g, Total Carbs: 0g, Net Carbs: 0g, Fiber: 0g, Protein: 0g; Sodium: 5mg

Macros: Fat: 98%, Carbs: 1%, Protein: 1%

Mediterranean Frittata

GLUTEN-FREE, NUT-FREE, VEGETARIAN

Serves 2
Prep Time: 10 minutes
Cook Time: 15 minutes

4 large eggs

2 tablespoons fresh
chopped herbs, such as
rosemary, thyme, oregano,
basil or 1 teaspoon
dried herbs

¼ teaspoon salt

Freshly ground black pepper

4 tablespoons extra-virgin
olive oil, divided

1 cup fresh spinach, arugula,
kale, or other leafy greens

4 ounces quartered
artichoke hearts,
rinsed, drained, and
thoroughly dried

8 cherry tomatoes, halved

½ cup crumbled soft
goat cheese

A frittata is an Italian egg dish, similar to an omelet but more versatile for any time of day. Full of fresh Mediterranean flavors and micronutrient-rich veggies and fresh herbs, this easy version is a great way to start your morning.

1. Preheat the oven to broil on low.

2. In small bowl, combine the eggs, herbs, salt, and pepper and whisk well with a fork. Set aside.

3. In a 4- to 5-inch oven-safe skillet or omelet pan, heat 2 tablespoons olive oil over medium heat. Add the spinach, artichoke hearts, and cherry tomatoes and sauté until just wilted, 1 to 2 minutes.

4. Pour in the egg mixture and let it cook undisturbed over medium heat for 3 to 4 minutes, until the eggs begin to set on the bottom.

5. Sprinkle the goat cheese across the top of the egg mixture and transfer the skillet to the oven.

6. Broil for 4 to 5 minutes, or until the frittata is firm in the center and golden brown on top.

7. Remove from the oven and run a rubber spatula around the edge to loosen the sides. Invert onto a large plate or cutting board and slice in half. Serve warm and drizzled with the remaining 2 tablespoons olive oil.

Per Serving: Calories: 527, Total Fat: 47g, Total Carbs: 10g, Net Carbs: 7g, Fiber: 3g, Protein: 21g; Sodium: 760mg

Macros: Fat: 79%, Carbs: 5%, Protein: 16%

Green Goddess Smoothie

DAIRY-FREE, EGG-FREE, GLUTEN-FREE, VEGAN

Serves 1
Prep Time: 5 minutes

1 small very ripe avocado,
    peeled and pitted
1 cup almond milk or water,
    plus more as needed
1 cup tender baby spinach
    leaves, stems removed
½ medium cucumber,
    peeled and seeded
1 tablespoon extra-virgin
    olive oil or avocado oil
8 to 10 fresh mint leaves,
    stems removed
Juice of 1 lime (about 1 to
    2 tablespoons)

Smoothies make for a quick and easy breakfast on the go, but so many "healthy" green smoothies are filled with sugars from juices, fruits, and other sweeteners, such as honey or maple syrup. This refreshing and filling version uses fresh mint, cucumber, and lime juice for a bold flavor without all the sugar. If you desire a sweeter taste, you can add a small amount of natural sugar-free sweetener to taste. You can also add a scoop of collagen powder (limit to 10g) for a good source of protein or try adding a hardboiled egg on the side for a heartier meal.

In a blender or a large wide-mouth jar, if using an immersion blender, combine the avocado, almond milk, spinach, cucumber, olive oil, mint, and lime juice and blend until smooth and creamy, adding more almond milk or water to achieve your desired consistency.

Substitution Tip: Feel free to substitute baby kale or Swiss chard for the baby spinach but look for more tender leaves to avoid a rougher texture.

Per Serving: Calories: 330, Total Fat: 30g, Total Carbs: 19g, Net Carbs: 10g, Fiber: 9g, Protein: 4g; Sodium: 36mg

Macros: Fat: 77%, Carbs: 19%, Protein: 4%

Blueberry Power Smoothie

DAIRY-FREE, EGG-FREE, GLUTEN-FREE, VEGAN

Serves 1
Prep Time: 5 minutes

1 cup unsweetened almond
    milk, plus more as needed
¼ cup frozen blueberries
2 tablespoons unsweetened
    almond butter
1 tablespoon ground
    flaxseed or chia seeds
1 tablespoon extra-virgin
    olive oil or avocado oil
1 to 2 teaspoons stevia
    or monk fruit extract
    (optional)
½ teaspoon vanilla extract
¼ teaspoon ground
    cinnamon

Dark berries—such as blueberries, blackberries, and raspberries—are high in antioxidants and can reduce inflammation and improve cardiovascular health. This recipe uses almond butter, but you can substitute cashew or macadamia nut butter for a naturally sweeter version. The sweetener is optional, but always aim for using as little as possible to allow your palate to appreciate the natural sweetness of the berries and nuts.

In a blender or a large wide-mouth jar, if using an immersion blender, combine the almond milk, blueberries, almond butter, flaxseed, olive oil, stevia (if using), vanilla, and cinnamon and blend until smooth and creamy, adding more almond milk to achieve your desired consistency.

Substitution Tip: I love using frozen berries for convenience, but feel free to use fresh if you have them. You can also substitute another berry, such as raspberries or strawberries, for the blueberries.

Per Serving: Calories: 460, Total Fat: 40g, Total Carbs: 20g, Net Carbs: 10g, Fiber: 10g, Protein: 9g; Sodium: 147mg

Macros: Fat: 78%, Carbs: 17%, Protein: 5%

Spiced Orange-Pistachio Smoothie

EGG-FREE, GLUTEN-FREE, VEGETARIAN

Serves 1
Prep Time: 5 minutes

½ cup plain whole-milk
   Greek yogurt
½ cup unsweetened almond
   milk, plus more as needed
Zest and juice of
   1 clementine or ½ orange
1 tablespoon extra-virgin
   olive oil or MCT oil
1 tablespoon
   shelled pistachios,
   coarsely chopped
1 to 2 teaspoons monk fruit
   extract or stevia (optional)
¼ to ½ teaspoon ground
   allspice or unsweetened
   pumpkin pie spice
¼ teaspoon ground
   cinnamon
¼ teaspoon vanilla extract

Fresh oranges paired with nuts and warm spices is a common flavor combination found in many desserts in the Mediterranean region. This smoothie is like a sophisticated version of an orange creamsicle, a treat that always reminds me of my childhood. With plenty of protein from yogurt, you don't need protein or collagen powders. The sweetener is optional—you can add extra orange zest or spices to increase flavor without it, if you prefer.

In a blender or a large wide-mouth jar, if using an immersion blender, combine the yogurt, ½ cup almond milk, clementine zest and juice, olive oil, pistachios, monk fruit extract (if using), allspice, cinnamon, and vanilla and blend until smooth and creamy, adding more almond milk to achieve your desired consistency.

Per Serving: Calories: 264, Total Fat: 22g, Total Carbs: 12g, Net Carbs: 10g, Fiber: 2g, Protein: 6g; Sodium: 127mg

Macros: Fat: 73%, Carbs: 17%, Protein: 10%

Florentine Breakfast Sandwich

GLUTEN-FREE, VEGETARIAN

Serves 1
Prep Time: 10 minutes
Cook Time: 5 minutes

1 teaspoon extra-virgin
   olive oil
1 large egg
¼ teaspoon salt
¼ teaspoon freshly ground
   black pepper
1 Versatile Sandwich Round
   (page 169)
1 tablespoon jarred pesto
¼ ripe avocado, mashed
1 (¼-inch) thick tomato slice
1 (1-ounce) slice fresh
   mozzarella

With classic Italian flavors of basil, mozzarella, and tomato, this filling breakfast sandwich will satisfy your taste buds as well as your appetite. Use a savory version of the Versatile Sandwich Round (page 169), such as rosemary and olive oil, or make your own version with whatever herbs you have on hand.

1. In a small skillet, heat the olive oil over high heat. When the oil is very hot, crack the egg into the skillet and reduce the heat to medium. Sprinkle the top of the egg with salt and pepper and let it cook for 2 minutes, or until set on bottom.

2. Using a spatula, flip the egg to cook on the other side to desired level of doneness (1 to 2 minutes for a runnier yolk, 2 to 3 minutes for a more set yolk). Remove the egg from the pan and keep warm.

3. Cut the sandwich round in half horizontally and toast, if desired.

4. To assemble the sandwich, spread the pesto on a toasted bread half. Top with mashed avocado, the tomato slice, mozzarella, and the cooked egg. Top with the other bread half and eat warm.

Substitution Tip: Fresh mozzarella really creates excellent texture and flavor, but feel free to substitutes a slice of provolone or Cheddar (or omit entirely) if you desire.

Per Serving: Calories: 548, Total Fat: 48g, Total Carbs: 8g, Net Carbs: 5g, Fiber: 3g, Protein: 21g; Sodium: 1450mg

Macros: Fat: 79%, Carbs: 6%, Protein: 15%

Avocado Toast

DAIRY-FREE, GLUTEN-FREE, NUT-FREE, VEGETARIAN

Serves 2
Prep Time: 5 minutes
Cook Time: 5 minutes

2 tablespoons ground
  flaxseed
½ teaspoon baking powder
2 large eggs
1 teaspoon salt, plus more
  for serving
½ teaspoon freshly ground
  black pepper, plus more
  for serving
½ teaspoon garlic powder,
  sesame seed, caraway
  seed or other dried herbs
  (optional)
3 tablespoons extra-virgin
  olive oil, divided
1 medium ripe avocado,
  peeled, pitted, and sliced
2 tablespoons chopped ripe
  tomato or salsa

Pan tostado is an easy breakfast popular in Spain. Typically topped with a tomato purée and drizzled with olive oil, it tends to be carbohydrate dense. This version uses an egg and flaxseed base for a twist on the avocado toast trend with healthy fats and decadent flavor. Top with your favorite hot sauce for a little kick.

1. In a small bowl, combine the flaxseed and baking powder, breaking up any lumps in the baking powder. Add the eggs, salt, pepper, and garlic powder (if using) and whisk well. Let sit for 2 minutes.

2. In a small nonstick skillet, heat 1 tablespoon olive oil over medium heat. Pour the egg mixture into the skillet and let cook undisturbed until the egg begins to set on bottom, 2 to 3 minutes.

3. Using a rubber spatula, scrape down the sides to allow uncooked egg to reach the bottom. Cook another 2 to 3 minutes.

4. Once almost set, flip like a pancake and allow the top to fully cook, another 1 to 2 minutes.

5. Remove from the pan and allow to cool slightly. Slice into 2 pieces.

6. Top each "toast" with avocado slices, additional salt and pepper, chopped tomato, and drizzle with the remaining 2 tablespoons olive oil.

Per Serving (1 toast): Calories: 287, Total Fat: 25g, Total Carbs: 10g, Net Carbs: 3g, Fiber: 7g, Protein: 9g; Sodium: 1130mg

Macros: Fat: 76%, Carbs: 12%, Protein: 12%

Baklava Hot Porridge

DAIRY-FREE, EGG-FREE, GLUTEN-FREE, VEGAN

Serves 2
Prep Time: 5 minutes
Cook Time: 5 minutes

2 cups Riced Cauliflower
   (page 177)
¾ cup unsweetened almond,
   flax, or hemp milk
4 tablespoons extra-virgin
   olive oil, divided
2 teaspoons grated fresh
   orange peel (from
   ½ orange)
½ teaspoon ground
   cinnamon
½ teaspoon almond extract
   or vanilla extract
⅛ teaspoon salt
4 tablespoons chopped
   walnuts, divided
1 to 2 teaspoons liquid
   stevia, monk fruit, or
   other sweetener of choice
   (optional)

Baklava is a classic Greek dessert made from phyllo dough filled with nuts and cinnamon and covered with a honey syrup. Inspired by this winning flavor combination, this hot breakfast porridge uses grain-free riced cauliflower and is loaded with the warm comforting flavors of nuts, orange, and spices without all the sugar. You can make your own Riced Cauliflower (page 177) or use store-bought preprepared riced cauliflower.

1. In medium saucepan, combine the riced cauliflower, almond milk, 2 tablespoons olive oil, grated orange peel, cinnamon, almond extract, and salt. Stir to combine and bring just to a boil over medium-high heat, stirring constantly.

2. Remove from heat and stir in 2 tablespoons chopped walnuts and sweetener (if using). Stir to combine.

3. Divide into bowls, topping each with 1 tablespoon of chopped walnuts and 1 tablespoon of the remaining olive oil.

Substitution Tip: You can use shelled pistachios or chopped pecans in place of the walnuts for a slightly sweeter taste.

Per Serving: Calories: 382, Total Fat: 38g, Total Carbs: 11g, Net Carbs: 7g, Fiber: 4g, Protein: 5g; Sodium: 229mg

Macros: Fat: 86%, Carbs: 10%, Protein: 4%

Lemon-Olive Oil Breakfast Cakes with Berry Syrup

DAIRY-FREE, GLUTEN-FREE, VEGETARIAN

Serves 4
Prep Time: 5 minutes
Cook Time: 10 minutes

For the Pancakes

1 cup almond flour
1 teaspoon baking powder
¼ teaspoon salt
6 tablespoon extra-virgin olive oil, divided
2 large eggs
Zest and juice of 1 lemon
½ teaspoon almond or vanilla extract

For the Berry Sauce

1 cup frozen mixed berries
1 tablespoon water or lemon juice, plus more if needed
½ teaspoon vanilla extract

Weekends are made for pancakes! Olive oil–based cakes are a common staple for the Mediterranean baker. The lemon flavor in these breakfast cakes is a light and refreshing new twist on a breakfast favorite.

To Make the Pancakes

1. In a large bowl, combine the almond flour, baking powder, and salt and whisk to break up any clumps.

2. Add the 4 tablespoons olive oil, eggs, lemon zest and juice, and almond extract and whisk to combine well.

3. In a large skillet, heat 1 tablespoon of olive oil and spoon about 2 tablespoons of batter for each of 4 pancakes. Cook until bubbles begin to form, 4 to 5 minutes, and flip. Cook another 2 to 3 minutes on second side. Repeat with remaining 1 tablespoon olive oil and batter.

To Make the Berry Sauce

In a small saucepan, heat the frozen berries, water, and vanilla extract over medium-high for 3 to 4 minutes, until bubbly, adding more water if mixture is too thick. Using the back of a spoon or fork, mash the berries and whisk until smooth.

Per Serving (2 pancakes with ¼ cup berry syrup):
Calories: 275, Total Fat: 26g, Total Carbs: 8g, Net Carbs: 6g, Fiber: 2g, Protein: 4g; Sodium: 271mg

Macros: Fat: 83%, Carbs: 11%, Protein: 6%

Greek Yogurt Parfait

EGG-FREE, GLUTEN-FREE, VEGETARIAN

Serves 1
Prep Time: 5 minutes

½ cup plain whole-milk
  Greek yogurt
2 tablespoons heavy
  whipping cream
¼ cup frozen berries,
  thawed with juices
½ teaspoon vanilla or
  almond extract (optional)
¼ teaspoon ground
  cinnamon (optional)
1 tablespoon ground
  flaxseed
2 tablespoons chopped nuts
  (walnuts or pecans)

This quick and easy breakfast on the go is full of satiating heart-healthy fats, quality protein, antioxidants, and probiotics for a happy tummy. You can use fresh berries in this parfait, but thawed frozen berries do a great job of naturally flavoring the plain yogurt as they thaw. I love frozen wild blueberries in this, but any small berry blend works well.

In a small bowl or glass, combine the yogurt, heavy whipping cream, thawed berries in their juice, vanilla or almond extract (if using), cinnamon (if using), and flaxseed and stir well until smooth. Top with chopped nuts and enjoy.

Substitution Tip: You could use chia seeds in place of the flaxseeds in this parfait for an equally powerful addition of healthy omega-3 fatty acids.

Per Serving: Calories: 267, Total Fat: 19g, Total Carbs: 12g, Net Carbs: 8g, Fiber: 4g, Protein: 12g; Sodium: 63mg

Macros: Fat: 65% Carbs: 17% Protein: 18%

Greek Egg and Tomato Scramble

GLUTEN-FREE, NUT-FREE, VEGETARIAN

Serves 4
Prep Time: 10 minutes
Cook Time: 25 minutes

¼ cup extra-virgin olive oil, divided

1 ½ cups chopped fresh tomatoes

¼ cup finely minced red onion

2 garlic cloves, minced

½ teaspoon dried oregano or 1 to 2 teaspoons chopped fresh oregano

½ teaspoon dried thyme or 1 to 2 teaspoons chopped fresh thyme

8 large eggs

½ teaspoon salt

¼ teaspoon freshly ground black pepper

¾ cup crumbled feta cheese

¼ cup chopped fresh mint leaves

Strapatsatha is a simple Greek breakfast dish of scrambled eggs with herbs and fresh tomatoes. Here it is made even more flavorful with the addition of mint and feta. This recipe calls for fresh tomato, making it ideal for summer months, but you can use canned tomatoes to enjoy this year-round. Add sautéed spinach or kale for an extra dose of micronutrients!

1. In large skillet, heat the olive oil over medium heat. Add the chopped tomatoes and red onion and sauté until tomatoes are cooked through and soft, 10 to 12 minutes.

2. Add the garlic, oregano, and thyme and sauté another 2 to 4 minutes, until fragrant and liquid has reduced.

3. In a medium bowl, whisk together the eggs, salt, and pepper until well combined.

4. Add the eggs to the skillet, reduce the heat to low, and scramble until set and creamy, using a spatula to move them constantly, 3 to 4 minutes. Remove the skillet from the heat, stir in the feta and mint, and serve warm.

Cooking Tip: For perfectly cooked, creamy scrambled eggs, make sure to cook the eggs over low heat, stirring constantly. Eggs cooked on higher heat will be drier and have a waxy finish.

Per Serving: Calories: 338, Total Fat: 28g, Total Carbs: 6g, Net Carbs: 5g, Fiber: 1g, Protein: 16g; Sodium: 570mg

Macros: Fat: 74%, Carbs: 7%, Protein: 19%

Egg Baked in Avocado

GLUTEN-FREE, VEGETARIAN

Serves 2
Prep Time: 5 minutes
Cook Time: 15 minutes

1 ripe large avocado

2 large eggs

Salt

Freshly ground black pepper

4 tablespoons jarred pesto,
  for serving

2 tablespoons chopped
  tomato, for serving

2 tablespoons crumbled
  feta, for serving (optional)

This is a fun new way to jazz up your morning egg routine. They are so pretty that they make a great addition to a brunch party. I like these with basil pesto, but any herby sauce, such as the Parsley Pistou (page 118), works nicely. These don't save very well, so make sure to only make what you're planning on eating in the moment.

1. Preheat the oven to 425°F.

2. Slice the avocado in half and remove the pit. Scoop out about 1 to 2 tablespoons from each half to create a hole large enough to fit an egg. Place the avocado halves on a baking sheet, cut-side up.

3. Crack 1 egg in each avocado half and season with salt and pepper.

4. Bake until the eggs are set and cooked to desired level of doneness, 10 to 15 minutes.

5. Remove from oven and top each avocado with 2 tablespoons pesto, 1 tablespoon chopped tomato, and 1 tablespoon crumbled feta (if using).

Per Serving: Calories: 302, Total Fat: 26g, Total Carbs: 10g, Net Carbs: 5g, Fiber: 5g, Protein: 8g; Sodium: 436mg

Macros: Fat: 75%, Carbs: 15%, Protein: 10%

Sweet 'n' Savory Toast with Burrata and Berries

GLUTEN-FREE, VEGETARIAN

Serves 2
Prep Time: 5 minutes

½ cup mixed frozen berries
Juice of 1 clementine or
  ½ orange (about ¼ cup)
½ teaspoon vanilla extract
1 Versatile Sandwich Round
  (page 169)
2 ounces burrata cheese

This dish is the perfect combination of textures. Burrata is a rich, buttery cheese from Italy, made from fresh mozzarella cheese stuffed with cream. It has gained popularity in the United States in recent years and can now be found at many grocery stores in the fresh cheese section. Use a sweeter Versatile Sandwich Round (page 169), such as cinnamon or plain, not herbed.

1. To make the berry sauce, in a small saucepan, heat the frozen berries, clementine juice, and vanilla over medium-high heat until simmering. Reduce the heat to low and simmer, stirring occasionally, until the liquid reduces and the mixture becomes syrupy.

2. Cut the sandwich round in half horizontally and toast each half in a toaster or under a broiler.

3. On a rimmed dish, slice the burrata into two slices, reserving the cream.

4. Top each toasted sandwich round half with 1 ounce sliced burrata cheese, the reserved cream, and ¼ cup berry sauce.

Substitution Tip: If you can't find burrata, you can substitute fresh ricotta for a similar texture in this recipe.

Per Serving (1 toast): Calories: 221, Total Fat: 17g, Total Carbs: 6g, Net Carbs: 5g, Fiber: 1g, Protein: 11g; Sodium: 225mg

Macros: Fat: 69%, Carbs: 11%, Protein: 20%

Crustless Greek Cheese Pie

GLUTEN-FREE, NUT-FREE, VEGETARIAN

Serves 6
Prep Time: 10 minutes
Cook Time: 40 minutes

4 tablespoons extra-virgin
olive oil, divided
1 ¼ cups crumbled
traditional Greek feta
½ cup whole-milk ricotta
2 tablespoons chopped
fresh mint
1 tablespoon chopped
fresh dill
½ teaspoon lemon zest
¼ teaspoon freshly ground
black pepper
2 large eggs
½ teaspoon baking powder

The *tiropita*, or Greek cheese pie, is a very traditional breakfast served at many cafes throughout the country. This crustless version is not only lower in carbohydrates and gluten free, but it takes a fraction of the time of the traditional version made with phyllo dough. Delicious with a cup of coffee in the morning, it can also be a light lunch alongside a Traditional Greek Salad (page 76).

1. Preheat the oven to 350°F.

2. Pour 2 tablespoons olive oil into an 8-inch square baking dish and swirl to coat the bottom and about 1 inch up the sides of the dish.

3. In a medium bowl, combine the feta and ricotta and blend well with a fork, crumbling the feta into very small pieces.

4. Stir in the mint, dill, lemon zest, and pepper and mix well.

5. In a small bowl, beat together the eggs and baking powder. Add to the cheese mixture and blend well.

6. Pour into the prepared baking dish and drizzle the remaining 2 tablespoons olive oil over top.

7. Bake until lightly browned and set, 35 to 40 minutes.

Per Serving: Calories: 182, Total Fat: 17g, Total Carbs: 2g, Net Carbs: 2g, Fiber: 0g, Protein: 7g; Sodium: 322mg

Macros: Fat: 82%, Carbs: 3%, Protein: 15%

CHAPTER FOUR

Snacks and Appetizers

Marinated Feta and Artichokes

EGG-FREE, GLUTEN-FREE, NUT-FREE, VEGETARIAN

Makes 1½ cups
Prep Time: 10 minutes,
plus 4 hours inactive time

4 ounces traditional
  Greek feta, cut into
  ½-inch cubes
4 ounces drained artichoke
  hearts, quartered
  lengthwise
⅓ cup extra-virgin olive oil
Zest and juice of 1 lemon
2 tablespoons roughly
  chopped fresh rosemary
2 tablespoons roughly
  chopped fresh parsley
½ teaspoon black
  peppercorns

Mezze, or tapas, are small snacks meant to be shared and enjoyed with friends and family over a glass of wine and laughter and are integral to Mediterranean culture. Along with many of the other recipes in this section, these can be made in advance, stored in the refrigerator until ready to enjoy, and served in combination with a few other small plates to create a social dining experience.

1. In a glass bowl or large glass jar, combine the feta and artichoke hearts. Add the olive oil, lemon zest and juice, rosemary, parsley, and peppercorns and toss gently to coat, being sure not to crumble the feta.

2. Cover and refrigerate for at least 4 hours, or up to 4 days. Pull out of the refrigerator 30 minutes before serving.

Substitution Tip: You can substitute small fresh mozzarella balls (*ciliegine*) or goat cheese formed into ½-inch balls in place of the feta, if you prefer. Similarly, you can mix up the herbs with whatever you have on hand.

Per Serving (⅓ cup): Calories: 235, Total Fat: 23g, Total Carbs: 3g, Net Carbs: 2g, Fiber: 1g, Protein: 4g; Sodium: 406mg

Macros: Fat: 88%, Carbs: 5%, Protein: 7%

Tuna Croquettes

Makes 36 croquettes
Prep Time: 40 minutes, plus hours to overnight to chill
Cook Time: 25 minutes

6 tablespoons extra-virgin olive oil, plus 1 to 2 cups

5 tablespoons almond flour, plus 1 cup, divided

1 ¼ cups heavy cream

1 (4-ounce) can olive oil-packed yellowfin tuna

1 tablespoon chopped red onion

2 teaspoons minced capers

½ teaspoon dried dill

¼ teaspoon freshly ground black pepper

2 large eggs

1 cup panko breadcrumbs (or a gluten-free version)

Go to Spain—eat your weight in *croquetas*. I fell in love with these crispy on the outside, warm and gooey in the inside little masterpieces that are found in virtually every restaurant, bar, and café throughout Spain. I have had fun experimenting with different variations throughout the years by changing up ingredients and spices and this keto-friendly version is just as tasty and addictive as the traditional recipes. They take a little time but are well worth the effort. You can swap out leftover ham or shredded cooked chicken for the tuna, add mushrooms or cooked spinach, and mix up the herbs to play around with different flavors—just keep the base and method the same.

1. In a large skillet, heat 6 tablespoons olive oil over medium-low heat. Add 5 tablespoons almond flour and cook, stirring constantly, until a smooth paste forms and the flour browns slightly, 2 to 3 minutes.

2. Increase the heat to medium-high and gradually add the heavy cream, whisking constantly until completely smooth and thickened, another 4 to 5 minutes.

3. Remove from the heat and stir in the tuna, red onion, capers, dill, and pepper.

4. Transfer the mixture to an 8-inch square baking dish that is well coated with olive oil and allow to cool to room temperature. Cover and refrigerate until chilled, at least 4 hours or up to overnight.

(Recipe continues)

Tuna Croquettes, continued

5. To form the croquettes, set out three bowls. In one, beat together the eggs. In another, add the remaining almond flour. In the third, add the panko. Line a baking sheet with parchment paper.

6. Using a spoon, place about a tablespoon of cold prepared dough into the flour mixture and roll to coat. Shake off excess and, using your hands, roll into an oval.

7. Dip the croquette into the beaten egg, then lightly coat in panko. Set on lined baking sheet and repeat with the remaining dough.

8. In a small saucepan, heat the remaining 1 to 2 cups of olive oil, so that the oil is about 1 inch deep, over medium-high heat. The smaller the pan, the less oil you will need, but you will need more for each batch.

9. Test if the oil is ready by throwing a pinch of panko into pot. If it sizzles, the oil is ready for frying. If it sinks, it's not quite ready. Once the oil is heated, fry the croquettes 3 or 4 at a time, depending on the size of your pan, removing with a slotted spoon when golden brown. You will need to adjust the temperature of the oil occasionally to prevent burning. If the croquettes get dark brown very quickly, lower the temperature.

Leftovers Tip: These are best served hot just after cooking, so only fry as many as you plan to eat. Left-over filling can be stored in the fridge for up to 3 days or frozen up to 3 months for later use.

Per Serving (3 croquettes): Calories: 245, Total Fat: 22g, Total Carbs: 7g, Net Carbs: 6g, Fiber: 1g, Protein: 6g; Sodium: 85mg

Macros: Fat: 78%, Carbs: 12%, Protein: 10%

Smoked Salmon Crudités

DAIRY-FREE, EGG-FREE, GLUTEN-FREE, NUT-FREE

Serves 4
Prep Time: 10 minutes

6 ounces smoked
   wild salmon
2 tablespoons Roasted
   Garlic Aioli (page 167) or
   avocado mayonnaise
1 tablespoon Dijon mustard
1 tablespoon chopped
   scallions, green parts only
2 teaspoons chopped capers
½ teaspoon dried dill
4 endive spears or hearts
   of romaine
½ English cucumber, cut
   into ¼-inch-thick rounds

Full of heart-healthy omega-3 fatty acids, this light dip is perfect served with fresh veggies such as the endive and cucumbers in this recipe, atop Seedy Crackers (page 181), or even as a light lunch with a fresh green salad. You can make extra at the beginning of the week to have as a quick snack or grab-and-go lunch. Always look for wild-caught salmon as opposed to farm-raised for the highest amount of omega-3s.

1. Roughly chop the smoked salmon and place in a small bowl. Add the aioli, Dijon, scallions, capers, and dill and mix well.

2. Top endive spears and cucumber rounds with a spoonful of smoked salmon mixture and enjoy chilled.

Substitution Tip: You can substitute canned salmon (removing bones and skin) or chipped sardines or mackerel for the smoked salmon, if you prefer.

Per Serving (1 crudité): Calories: 92, Total Fat: 5g, Total Carbs: 5g, Net Carbs: 4g, Fiber: 1g, Protein: 9g; Sodium: 472mg

Macros: Fat: 44%, Carbs: 18%, Protein: 38%

Citrus-Marinated Olives

DAIRY-FREE, EGG-FREE, GLUTEN-FREE, NUT-FREE, VEGAN

Makes 2 cups
Prep Time: 10 minutes,
plus 4 hours to marinate

2 cups mixed green olives
   with pits
¼ cup red wine vinegar
¼ cup extra-virgin olive oil
4 garlic cloves, finely minced
Zest and juice of
   2 clementines or
   1 large orange
1 teaspoon red pepper flakes
2 bay leaves
½ teaspoon ground cumin
½ teaspoon ground allspice

Inspired by North African flavors, the slightly sweet and spicy combination of these olives truly is unique. The longer these olives marinate, the deeper their flavor, so if you have the time, give them at least a few days in the refrigerator before serving. These can also be heated right before serving for a warm and savory treat.

In a large glass bowl or jar, combine the olives, vinegar, oil, garlic, orange zest and juice, red pepper flakes, bay leaves, cumin, and allspice and mix well. Cover and refrigerate for at least 4 hours or up to a week to allow the olives to marinate, tossing again before serving.

Per Serving (¼ cup): Calories: 133, Total Fat: 14g, Total Carbs: 3g, Net Carbs: 1g, Fiber: 2g, Protein: 1g; Sodium: 501mg

Macros: Fat: 88%, Carbs: 10%, Protein: 2%

Olive Tapenade with Anchovies

DAIRY-FREE, GLUTEN-FREE, NUT-FREE

Makes 2 cups
Prep Time: 10 minutes,
plus 1 hour to marinate

2 cups pitted Kalamata
olives or other black olives
2 anchovy fillets, chopped
2 teaspoons chopped capers
1 garlic clove, finely minced
1 cooked egg yolk
1 teaspoon Dijon mustard
¼ cup extra-virgin olive oil
Seedy Crackers (page 181),
Versatile Sandwich Round
(page 169), or vegetables,
for serving (optional)

This tapenade, or spread, has a wonderfully salty umami flavor and is an excellent addition to a tapas or mezze platter. It is also a great condiment for cooked meat or eggs. Not everyone is an anchovy fan, but this is an excellent way to introduce them into your diet and get a great dose of omega-3 fatty acids. You can use green olives, if you prefer them to black.

1. Rinse the olives in cold water and drain well.

2. In a food processor, blender, or a large jar (if using an immersion blender) place the drained olives, anchovies, capers, garlic, egg yolk, and Dijon. Process until it forms a thick paste.

3. With the food processor running, slowly stream in the olive oil.

4. Transfer to a small bowl, cover, and refrigerate at least 1 hour to let the flavors develop. Serve with Seedy Crackers (page 181), atop a Versatile Sandwich Round (page 169), or with your favorite crunchy vegetables.

Prep Tip: With all of the naturally salty ingredients in this recipe, soaking the olives briefly before blending them into this dip will help cut back on the salt flavor.

Per Serving (⅓ cup): Calories: 179, Total Fat: 19g, Total Carbs: 3g, Net Carbs: 1g, Fiber: 2g, Protein: 2g; Sodium: 812mg

Macros: Fat: 92%, Carbs: 5%, Protein: 3%

Greek Deviled Eggs

GLUTEN-FREE, NUT-FREE, VEGETARIAN

Serves 4

Prep Time: 15 minutes, plus 30 minutes to chill

Cook Time: 15 minutes

4 large hardboiled eggs

2 tablespoons Roasted Garlic Aioli (page 167) or whole-milk Greek yogurt

½ cup finely crumbled feta cheese

8 pitted Kalamata olives, finely chopped

2 tablespoons chopped sun-dried tomatoes

1 tablespoon minced red onion

½ teaspoon dried dill

¼ teaspoon freshly ground black pepper

Deviled eggs make a great grab-and-go snack, or you can enjoy them with a Traditional Greek Salad (page 76) for a quick and easy midweek lunch. Place the filling into a piping bag to create a "fancier" egg but, with the pretty colors in these eggs, I find that simply spooning the yolk mixture into the whites gets the job done. Not only do fresh eggs deliver the highest nutritional value, they also peel much easier than eggs that have sat on a grocery store shelf for weeks. Getting fresh eggs from your local farmers' market is always the best way to go.

1. Slice the hardboiled eggs in half lengthwise, remove the yolks, and place the yolks in a medium bowl. Reserve the egg white halves and set aside.

2. Smash the yolks well with a fork. Add the aioli, feta, olives, sun-dried tomatoes, onion, dill, and pepper and stir to combine until smooth and creamy.

3. Spoon the filling into each egg white half and chill for 30 minutes, or up to 24 hours, covered.

Cooking Tip: For the perfect hardboiled egg, bring a large pot of water to a boil before adding the eggs. Carefully place the eggs in the boiling water and boil for 15 minutes. Remove from the heat and immediately drain, running cool water over the eggs. Cover with ice or very cold water until cool to the touch. Peel and enjoy!

Per Serving: Calories: 147, Total Fat: 11g, Total Carbs: 3g, Net Carbs: 3g, Fiber: 0g, Protein: 9g; Sodium: 334mg

Macros: Fat: 68%, Carbs: 9%, Protein: 23%

Manchego Crackers

GLUTEN-FREE, VEGETARIAN

Makes 40 crackers
Prep Time: 15 minutes,
plus 1 hour to chill dough
Cook Time: 15 minutes

Manchego is a sheep's milk cheese that you will find on almost every tapas menu throughout Spain. Enjoy these crackers with Olive Tapenade with Anchovies (page 59).

4 tablespoons butter, at room
   temperature
1 cup finely shredded
   Manchego cheese
1 cup almond flour
1 teaspoon salt, divided
¼ teaspoon freshly ground
   black pepper
1 large egg

1. Using an electric mixer, cream together the butter and shredded cheese until well combined and smooth.

2. In a small bowl, combine the almond flour with ½ teaspoon salt and pepper. Slowly add the almond flour mixture to the cheese, mixing constantly until the dough just comes together to form a ball.

3. Transfer to a piece of parchment or plastic wrap and roll into a cylinder log about 1½ inches thick. Wrap tightly and refrigerate for at least 1 hour.

4. Preheat the oven to 350°F. Line two baking sheets with parchment paper or silicone baking mats.

5. To make the egg wash, in a small bowl, whisk together the egg and remaining ½ teaspoon salt.

6. Slice the refrigerated dough into small rounds, about ¼ inch thick, and place on the lined baking sheets.

7. Brush the tops of the crackers with egg wash and bake until the crackers are golden and crispy, 12 to 15 minutes. Remove from the oven and allow to cool on a wire rack.

8. Serve warm or, once fully cooled, store in an airtight container in the refrigerator for up to 1 week.

Per Serving (10 crackers): Calories: 243, Total Fat: 23g, Total Carbs: 2g, Net Carbs: 1g, Fiber: 1g, Protein: 8g; Sodium: 792mg

Macros: Fat: 83%, Carbs: 4%, Protein: 13%

Burrata Caprese Stack

EGG-FREE, GLUTEN-FREE, NUT-FREE, VEGETARIAN

Serves 4

Prep Time: 5 minutes

1 large organic tomato,
  preferably heirloom
½ teaspoon salt
¼ teaspoon freshly ground
  black pepper
1 (4-ounce) ball
  burrata cheese
8 fresh basil leaves,
  thinly sliced
2 tablespoons extra-virgin
  olive oil
1 tablespoon red wine or
  balsamic vinegar

A traditional Italian caprese salad uses fresh mozzarella, ripe fresh tomatoes, basil, olive oil, and sometimes a drizzle of balsamic vinegar. This spin takes advantage of rich and creamy burrata cheese to increase the ratio of fat to protein and makes a fun little stacked Italian flag. Because burrata is so creamy, it goes on top of the thick tomato and is best eaten with a fork.

1. Slice the tomato into 4 thick slices, removing any tough center core and sprinkle with salt and pepper. Place the tomatoes, seasoned-side up, on a plate.

2. On a separate rimmed plate, slice the burrata into 4 thick slices and place one slice on top of each tomato slice. Top each with one-quarter of the basil and pour any reserved burrata cream from the rimmed plate over top.

3. Drizzle with olive oil and vinegar and serve with a fork and knife.

Substitution Tip: If you can't find burrata, you can use fresh mozzarella and drizzle with an additional 2 tablespoons olive oil.

Per Serving (1 stack): Calories: 153, Total Fat: 13g, Total Carbs: 2g, Net Carbs: 1g, Fiber: 1g, Protein: 7g; Sodium: 469mg

Macros: Fat: 76%, Carbs: 6%, Protein: 18%

Zucchini-Ricotta Fritters with Lemon-Garlic Aioli

GLUTEN-FREE, NUT-FREE, VEGETARIAN

Serves 4
Prep Time: 10 minutes, plus 20 minutes rest time
Cook Time: 25 minutes

1 large or 2 small/medium
   zucchini (about 2 cups
   drained, shredded)
1 teaspoon salt, divided
½ cup whole-milk
   ricotta cheese
2 scallions, both white and
   green parts, chopped
1 large egg
2 garlic cloves, finely minced
2 tablespoons chopped
   fresh mint (optional)
2 teaspoons grated
   lemon zest
¼ teaspoon freshly ground
   black pepper
½ cup almond flour
1 teaspoon baking powder
8 tablespoons extra-virgin
   olive oil
8 tablespoons Roasted
   Garlic Aioli (page 167) or
   avocado oil mayonnaise

These light and fresh fritters are a great way to jazz up zucchini. With protein from the ricotta and egg, they can even fill in as a light lunch or hearty breakfast. Draining the zucchini before making the batter is important or these little guys will go from light and crispy to soggy and heavy in a flash. Serve with Roasted Garlic Aioli (page 167) or a dollop of plain, whole-milk Greek yogurt.

1.   Place the shredded zucchini in a colander or on several layers of paper towels. Sprinkle with ½ teaspoon salt and let sit for 10 minutes. Using another layer of paper towels, press down on the zucchini to release any excess moisture and pat dry. Don't skip this step or your fritters will be soggy.

2.   In a large bowl, combine the drained zucchini, ricotta, scallions, egg, garlic, mint (if using), lemon zest, remaining ½ teaspoon salt, and pepper and stir well.

3.   In a small bowl, whisk together the almond flour and baking powder. Stir the flour mixture into the zucchini mixture and let rest for 10 minutes.

(Recipe continues)

Zucchini-Ricotta Fritters with Lemon-Garlic Aioli, continued

4. In a large skillet, working in four batches, fry the fritters. For each batch of four, heat 2 tablespoons olive oil over medium-high heat. Add 1 heaping tablespoon of zucchini batter per fritter, pressing down with the back of a spoon to form 2- to 3-inch fritters. Cover and let fry 2 minutes before flipping. Fry another 2 to 3 minutes, covered, or until crispy and golden and cooked through. You may need to reduce heat to medium to prevent burning. Remove from the pan and keep warm.

5. Repeat for the remaining three batches, using 2 tablespoons of the olive oil for each batch.

6. Serve fritters warm with aioli.

Substitution Tip: I love the mint flavor in warmer months, but you could substitute fresh sage or rosemary for a more autumn-inspired flavor.

Per Serving (4 fritters with 2 tablespoons aioli):
Calories: 448, Total Fat: 42g, Total Carbs: 12g, Net Carbs: 10g, Fiber: 2g, Protein: 8g; Sodium: 713mg

Macros: Fat: 84%, Carbs: 10%, Protein: 6%

Salmon-Stuffed Cucumbers

DAIRY-FREE, EGG-FREE, GLUTEN-FREE, NUT-FREE

Serves 4
Prep Time: 10 minutes

2 large cucumbers, peeled

1 (4-ounce) can red salmon

1 medium very ripe
avocado, peeled, pitted,
and mashed

1 tablespoon extra-virgin
olive oil

Zest and juice of 1 lime

3 tablespoons chopped
fresh cilantro

½ teaspoon salt

¼ teaspoon freshly ground
black pepper

As close to sushi as the Mediterranean Diet gets, these are a fun way to dress up seafood salad and are so cute in a lunch box that even kids will love them. Canned salmon is full of heart-healthy fats and low in mercury, but you could substitute leftover chopped cooked chicken or canned tuna if you prefer. Pop one or two for a quick snack full of satiating fats and quality proteins or turn four to six of them into an easy lunch. Cilantro adds great flavor, but feel free to omit it if you're not a fan.

1. Slice the cucumber into 1-inch-thick segments and using a spoon, scrape seeds out of center of each segment and stand up on a plate.

2. In a medium bowl, combine the salmon, avocado, olive oil, lime zest and juice, cilantro, salt, and pepper and mix until creamy.

3. Spoon the salmon mixture into the center of each cucumber segment and serve chilled.

Per Serving: Calories: 159, Total Fat: 11g, Total Carbs: 8g, Net Carbs: 5g, Fiber: 3g, Protein: 9g; Sodium: 398mg

Macros: Fat: 60%, Carbs: 19%, Protein: 21%

Goat Cheese–Mackerel Pâté

EGG-FREE, GLUTEN-FREE, NUT-FREE

Serves 4

Prep Time: 10 minutes

4 ounces olive oil-packed
   wild-caught mackerel

2 ounces goat cheese

Zest and juice of 1 lemon

2 tablespoons chopped
   fresh parsley

2 tablespoons chopped
   fresh arugula

1 tablespoon extra-virgin
   olive oil

2 teaspoons chopped capers

1 to 2 teaspoons fresh
   horseradish (optional)

Crackers, cucumber rounds,
   endive spears, or celery,
   for serving (optional)

Pâté is typically made from organ meats, which, while very nutrient dense, may not appeal to everyone. This version uses canned mackerel, which is lower in mercury than tuna and a great source of omega-3 fatty acids. Canned fish is a staple in Mediterranean cuisine, and varieties other than tuna can now be found at many grocery stores here in the United States. Look for wild-caught varieties canned in olive oil, if possible. Serve on Seedy Crackers (page 181) or make a sandwich with a savory Versatile Sandwich Round (page 169) for a heartier meal.

1. In a food processor, blender, or large bowl with immersion blender, combine the mackerel, goat cheese, lemon zest and juice, parsley, arugula, olive oil, capers, and horseradish (if using). Process or blend until smooth and creamy.

2. Serve with crackers, cucumber rounds, endive spears, or celery.

3. Store covered in the refrigerator for up to 1 week.

Substitution Tip: You can substitute cream cheese for the goat cheese if you aren't partial to the unique flavor of goat cheese.

Per Serving: Calories: 118, Total Fat: 8g, Total Carbs: 1g, Net Carbs: 1g, Fiber: 0g, Protein: 9g; Sodium: 196mg

Macros: Fat: 63%, Carbs: 4%, Protein: 33%

Taste of the Mediterranean Fat Bombs

EGG-FREE, GLUTEN-FREE, VEGETARIAN

Makes 6 fat bombs
Prep Time: 15 minutes, plus 4 hours to chill

1 cup crumbled goat cheese
4 tablespoons jarred pesto
12 pitted Kalamata olives, finely chopped
½ cup finely chopped walnuts
1 tablespoon chopped fresh rosemary

Fat bombs are a popular snack among those following a ketogenic diet and many people use them as an easy way to increase their fat ratios. However, not all fat bombs are created equal! It's important to have a high ratio of fat to protein and minimal carbs, so often there are extra sources of pure fats added in. Unfortunately, most fat bomb recipes use saturated fats in a solid state, such as coconut oil or butter, as their base. This version uses the heart-healthy fats in olive oil, olives, and walnuts to keep saturated fat ratios in check and serving them cold allows them to stay firm.

1. In a medium bowl, combine the goat cheese, pesto, and olives and mix well using a fork. Place in the refrigerator for at least 4 hours to harden.

2. Using your hands, form the mixture into 6 balls, about ¾-inch diameter. The mixture will be sticky.

3. In a small bowl, place the walnuts and rosemary and roll the goat cheese balls in the nut mixture to coat.

4. Store the fat bombs in the refrigerator for up to 1 week or in the freezer for up to 1 month.

Per Serving (1 fat bomb): Calories: 166, Total Fat: 15g, Total Carbs: 4g, Net Carbs: 3g, Fiber: 1g, Protein: 5g; Sodium: 337mg

Macros: Fat: 78%, Carbs: 10%, Protein: 12%

CHAPTER FIVE

Salads, Soups, and Sandwiches

Powerhouse Arugula Salad

EGG-FREE, GLUTEN-FREE, VEGETARIAN

Serves 4
Prep Time: 10 minutes

4 tablespoons extra-virgin
   olive oil
Zest and juice of
   2 clementines or 1 orange
   (2 to 3 tablespoons)
1 tablespoon red
   wine vinegar
½ teaspoon salt
¼ teaspoon freshly ground
   black pepper
8 cups baby arugula
1 cup coarsely
   chopped walnuts
1 cup crumbled goat cheese
½ cup pomegranate seeds

This salad has it all. It's crunchy, creamy, colorful, and packed with nutrition. Simple enough for a midweek lunch and pretty enough for entertaining, it will quickly become a favorite go-to. Tender peppery arugula, also known as "rocket" in Europe, is rated one of the top 20 nutrient-dense foods, with a very high vitamin and mineral content in relation to its caloric value. A great source of vitamins A, K, and C, folate, and the electrolyte minerals calcium and potassium, it is a wonderful vegetable to help combat the symptoms of "keto flu" (see page 10).

1. In a small bowl, whisk together the olive oil, zest and juice, vinegar, salt, and pepper and set aside.

2. To assemble the salad for serving, in a large bowl, combine the arugula, walnuts, goat cheese, and pomegranate seeds. Drizzle with the dressing and toss to coat.

Prep Tip: You can prep all the ingredients ahead of time, including the dressing. Store them in individual containers in the refrigerator and quickly toss together for an easy midweek salad. Add leftover fish, chicken, or a hardboiled egg to make a heartier meal.

Per Serving: Calories: 444, Total Fat: 40g, Total Carbs: 11g, Net Carbs: 8g, Fiber: 3g, Protein: 10g; Sodium: 412mg

Macros: Fat: 81%, Carbs: 10%, Protein: 9%

Cream of Cauliflower Gazpacho

DAIRY-FREE, EGG-FREE, GLUTEN-FREE, VEGAN

Serves 4 to 6
Prep Time: 15 minutes
Cook Time: 25 minutes

1 cup raw almonds

½ teaspoon salt

½ cup extra-virgin olive oil,
   plus 1 tablespoon, divided

1 small white onion, minced

1 small head cauliflower,
   stalk removed and broken
   into florets (about 3 cups)

2 garlic cloves, finely minced

2 cups chicken or vegetable
   stock or broth, plus more
   if needed

1 tablespoon red
   wine vinegar

¼ teaspoon freshly ground
   black pepper

Each region in Spain has its favorite style of gazpacho, the traditional cold soup of Spain. A creamy white version using almonds, garlic, and leftover bread is popular in Malaga, a port city in Southern Spain with rich culinary influences from North Africa. My version substitutes cauliflower for the bread, can be served warm or cold, and is rich with the Moorish flavor that defines the cuisine of the region. Blanching the almonds and removing the skin creates a silky smooth texture. In Spain, Marcona almonds, which are blanched almonds tossed in olive oil and salt, are a common snack and are to die for. You can find them at gourmet grocery stores in the United States but they are typically pretty pricy, so I recommend making your own as outlined here.

1. Bring a small pot of water to a boil. Add the almonds to the water and boil for 1 minute, being careful to not boil longer or the almonds will become soggy. Drain in a colander and run under cold water. Pat dry and, using your fingers, squeeze the meat of each almond out of its skin. Discard the skins.

2. In a food processor or blender, blend together the almonds and salt. With the processor running, drizzle in ½ cup extra-virgin olive oil, scraping down the sides as needed. Set the almond paste aside.

(Recipe continues)

3. In a large stockpot, heat the remaining 1 tablespoon olive oil over medium-high heat. Add the onion and sauté until golden, 3 to 4 minutes. Add the cauliflower florets and sauté for another 3 to 4 minutes. Add the garlic and sauté for 1 minute more.

4. Add 2 cups stock and bring to a boil. Cover, reduce the heat to medium-low, and simmer the vegetables until tender, 8 to 10 minutes. Remove from the heat and allow to cool slightly.

5. Add the vinegar and pepper. Using an immersion blender, blend until smooth. Alternatively, you can blend in a stand blender, but you may need to divide the mixture into two or three batches. With the blender running, add the almond paste and blend until smooth, adding extra stock if the soup is too thick.

6. Serve warm, or chill in refrigerator at least 4 to 6 hours to serve a cold gazpacho.

Substitution Tip: For ease, you can substitute prepared almond butter for the blanched almonds, but it will have more of a fibrous texture and be less smooth, due to the skins in the almond butter.

Per Serving: Calories: 505, Total Fat: 45g, Total Carbs: 15g, Net Carbs: 10g, Fiber: 5g, Protein: 10g; Sodium: 484mg

Macros: Fat: 80%, Carbs: 12%, Protein: 8%

Avocado Gazpacho

EGG-FREE, GLUTEN-FREE, NUT-FREE, VEGETARIAN

Serves 4
Prep Time: 15 minutes

2 cups chopped tomatoes

2 large ripe avocados, halved
and pitted

1 large cucumber, peeled
and seeded

1 medium bell pepper (red,
orange or yellow), chopped

1 cup plain whole-milk
Greek yogurt

¼ cup extra-virgin olive oil

¼ cup chopped fresh
cilantro

¼ cup chopped scallions,
green part only

2 tablespoons red
wine vinegar

Juice of 2 limes or 1 lemon

½ to 1 teaspoon salt

¼ teaspoon freshly ground
black pepper

Gazpacho is the classic cold soup of southern Spain. Spaniards never like to waste food, and traditional gazpacho uses day-old bread as its base to give the soup a great texture. This version uses the creaminess of pureed avocado rather than bread to create a creamy and hearty soup full of flavor and nutrition without gluten or excess carbohydrates. It works well as a starter course, light lunch, or even an on-the-go savory breakfast smoothie. The acid from the lime in this soup will help slow the browning of the avocado, but I still suggest eating this within 1 to 2 days.

1. In a blender or in a large bowl, if using an immersion blender, combine the tomatoes, avocados, cucumber, bell pepper, yogurt, olive oil, cilantro, scallions, vinegar, and lime juice. Blend until smooth. If using a stand blender, you may need to blend in two or three batches.

2. Season with salt and pepper and blend to combine the flavors.

3. Chill in the refrigerator for 1 to 2 hours before serving. Serve cold.

Prep Tip: To seed a cucumber, cut a peeled cucumber in half widthwise. Quarter each half lengthwise and stand each quarter on its end. Cut the knife down the length of the seeded side to remove the seeds.

Per Serving: Calories: 392, Total Fat: 32g, Total Carbs: 20g, Net Carbs: 11g, Fiber: 9g, Protein: 6g; Sodium: 335mg

Macros: Fat: 73%, Carbs: 20%, Protein: 7%

Tuscan Kale Salad with Anchovies

EGG-FREE, GLUTEN-FREE

Serves 4

Prep Time: 15 minutes, plus 30 minutes to rest

1 large bunch lacinato or dinosaur kale

¼ cup toasted pine nuts

1 cup shaved or coarsely shredded fresh Parmesan cheese

¼ cup extra-virgin olive oil

8 anchovy fillets, roughly chopped

2 to 3 tablespoons freshly squeezed lemon juice (from 1 large lemon)

2 teaspoons red pepper flakes (optional)

This simple salad is so full of flavor that it will wow dinner guests. Lacinato, or dinosaur kale, the darker tender green with long narrow leaves, is popular in Tuscany and works best in this salad, but you can substitute baby kale if you can't find it. Not everyone is an anchovy lover, but these little fish are packed with omega-3 fatty acids and add a wonderfully salty element to this salad that really can't be beat.

1. Remove the rough center stems from the kale leaves and roughly tear each leaf into about 4-by-1-inch strips. Place the torn kale in a large bowl and add the pine nuts and cheese.

2. In a small bowl, whisk together the olive oil, anchovies, lemon juice, and red pepper flakes (if using). Drizzle over the salad and toss to coat well. Let sit at room temperature 30 minutes before serving, tossing again just prior to serving.

Prep Tip: To easily remove the stem from each kale leaf, hold the leaf upside-down by the stem in one hand. With the other hand, grab the tender leaf around the base of the stem and gently pull down towards the tip. Discard the stem.

Per Serving: Calories: 337, Total Fat: 25g, Total Carbs: 12g, Net Carbs: 10g, Fiber: 2g, Protein: 16g; Sodium: 603mg

Macros: Fat: 67%, Carbs: 14%, Protein: 19%

Dilled Tuna Salad Sandwich

DAIRY-FREE, GLUTEN-FREE, NUT-FREE

Serves 4

Prep Time: 10 minutes

4 Versatile Sandwich
Rounds (page 169)

2 (4-ounce) cans tuna,
packed in olive oil

2 tablespoons Roasted
Garlic Aioli (page 167), or
avocado oil mayonnaise
with 1 to 2 teaspoons
freshly squeezed lemon
juice and/or zest

1 very ripe avocado, peeled,
pitted, and mashed

1 tablespoon chopped fresh
capers (optional)

1 teaspoon chopped fresh
dill or ½ teaspoon
dried dill

Canned tuna fish is such a wonderfully convenient way to get quality protein and is full of heart-healthy omega-3 fatty acids. I like to keep a can or two in the pantry at all times for those last-minute meals that don't require a trip to the grocery store. Look for sustainably wild-caught tuna packed in olive oil for lower mercury content and deeper flavor. You'll never buy tuna packed in water again!

1. Make sandwich rounds according to recipe. Cut each round in half and set aside.

2. In a medium bowl, place the tuna and the oil from cans. Add the aioli, avocado, capers (if using), and dill and blend well with a fork.

3. Toast sandwich rounds and fill each with one-quarter of the tuna salad, about ⅓ cup.

Leftovers Tip: This salad is delicious atop mixed greens, endive spears, hearts of romaine, or even enjoyed on its own.

Per Serving (1 sandwich): Calories: 436, Total Fat: 36g, Total Carbs: 5g, Net Carbs: 2g, Fiber: 3g, Protein: 23g; Sodium: 790mg

Macros: Fat: 74%, Carbs: 5%, Protein: 21%

Traditional Greek Salad

EGG-FREE, GLUTEN-FREE, NUT-FREE, VEGETARIAN

Serves 4
Prep Time: 10 minutes

2 large English cucumbers

4 Roma tomatoes, quartered

1 green bell pepper, cut into 1- to 1½-inch chunks

¼ small red onion, thinly sliced

4 ounces pitted Kalamata olives

¼ cup extra-virgin olive oil

2 tablespoons freshly squeezed lemon juice

1 tablespoon red wine vinegar

1 tablespoon chopped fresh oregano or 1 teaspoon dried oregano

¼ teaspoon freshly ground black pepper

4 ounces crumbled traditional feta cheese

One of my favorite clients that I have been working with for years grew up on traditional Greek cuisine and describes this as a salad without all the "fluff" (aka lettuce). This is best with a big hunk of salty feta cheese, but you can make it dairy-free by leaving it out. Beautiful in color and full of healthy fats, this is a great light lunch or dinner on its own or you can serve it alongside grilled fish or roasted meat.

1. Cut the cucumbers in half lengthwise and then into ½-inch-thick half-moons. Place in a large bowl.

2. Add the quartered tomatoes, bell pepper, red onion, and olives.

3. In a small bowl, whisk together the olive oil, lemon juice, vinegar, oregano, and pepper. Drizzle over the vegetables and toss to coat.

4. Divide between salad plates and top each with 1 ounce of feta.

Per Serving: Calories: 278, Total Fat: 22g, Total Carbs: 12g, Net Carbs: 8g, Fiber: 4g, Protein: 8g; Sodium: 572mg

Macros: Fat: 71%, Carbs: 16%, Protein: 13%

Crab Cake Lettuce Cups

DAIRY-FREE, GLUTEN-FREE

Serves 4

Prep Time: 25 minutes,
plus 15 minutes to marinate

Cook Time: 20 minutes

1 pound jumbo lump crab

1 large egg

6 tablespoons Roasted
Garlic Aioli (page
167) or avocado oil
mayonnaise, divided

2 tablespoons Dijon mustard

½ cup almond flour

¼ cup minced red onion

2 teaspoons smoked paprika

1 teaspoon celery salt

1 teaspoon garlic powder

1 teaspoon dried dill
(optional)

½ teaspoon freshly ground
black pepper

¼ cup extra-virgin olive oil

4 large Bibb lettuce leaves,
thick spine removed

Crab cakes may seem like an intimidating meal to master, but these come together in a flash. Crab claw meat or canned salmon, skin and bones removed, can be used in place of the more expensive jumbo lump crabmeat.

1. Place the crabmeat in a large bowl and pick out any visible shells, then break apart the meat with a fork.

2. In a small bowl, whisk together the egg, 2 tablespoons aioli, and Dijon mustard. Add to the crabmeat and blend with a fork. Add the almond flour, red onion, paprika, celery salt, garlic powder, dill (if using), and pepper and combine well. Let sit at room temperature for 10 to 15 minutes.

3. Form into 8 small cakes, about 2 inches in diameter.

4. In large skillet, heat the olive oil over medium-high heat. Fry the cakes until browned, 2 to 3 minutes per side. Cover the skillet, reduce the heat to low, and cook for another 6 to 8 minutes, or until set in the center. Remove from the skillet.

5. To serve, wrap 2 small crab cakes in each lettuce leaf and top with 1 tablespoon aioli.

Per Serving (2 crab cakes): Calories: 344, Total Fat: 24g, Total Carbs: 8g, Net Carbs: 6g, Fiber: 2g, Protein: 24g; Sodium: 615mg

Macros: Fat: 63%, Carbs: 9%, Protein: 28%

Orange-Tarragon Chicken Salad Wrap

EGG-FREE, GLUTEN-FREE

Serves 4

Prep Time: 15 minutes

½ cup plain whole-milk
   Greek yogurt

2 tablespoons Dijon mustard

2 tablespoons extra-virgin
   olive oil

2 tablespoons chopped
   fresh tarragon or
   1 teaspoon dried tarragon

½ teaspoon salt

¼ teaspoon freshly ground
   black pepper

2 cups cooked
   shredded chicken

½ cup slivered almonds

4 to 8 large Bibb
   lettuce leaves, tough
   stem removed

2 small ripe avocados,
   peeled and thinly sliced

Zest of 1 clementine, or
   ½ small orange (about
   1 tablespoon)

Fresh orange and tarragon spruce up tired chicken salad in these easy lunch wraps. I love the unique flavor the tarragon brings to this salad, but you can substitute another fresh herb, such as mint or basil. Make the chicken salad ahead of time and store in the refrigerator for a grab-and-go lunch or snack but wait to add the almonds until right before serving so they don't lose their crunch.

1. In a medium bowl, combine the yogurt, mustard, olive oil, tarragon, orange zest, salt, and pepper and whisk until creamy.

2. Add the shredded chicken and almonds and stir to coat.

3. To assemble the wraps, place about ½ cup chicken salad mixture in the center of each lettuce leaf and top with sliced avocados.

Per Serving: Calories: 440, Total Fat: 32g, Total Carbs: 12g, Net Carbs: 4g, Fiber: 8g, Protein: 26g; Sodium: 445mg

Macros: Fat: 65%, Carbs: 11%, Protein: 24%

Caprese Grilled Cheese

GLUTEN-FREE, VEGETARIAN

Serves 4
Prep Time: 10 minutes
Cook Time: 10 minutes

4 Versatile Sandwich
  Rounds (page 169)
8 tablespoons jarred pesto
4 ounces fresh mozzarella
  cheese, cut into
  4 round slices
1 Roma tomato or small
  slicing tomato, cut into
  4 slices
4 tablespoons extra-virgin
  olive oil

What is better than a perfectly grilled cheese sandwich, crispy on the outside and gooey on the inside with warm, melted cheese? Use fresh mozzarella and herby pesto for an out-of-this-world flavor combination that will warm your belly and wake up your taste buds! Serve alongside a mixed greens salad dressed with Simple Vinaigrette (page 170) for a quick and easy light dinner.

1. Slice each sandwich round in half horizontally and place, cut-side up, on a large cutting board.

2. Spread 1 tablespoon pesto over each half. Top 4 of the rounds with a mozzarella slice and tomato slice and close with the remaining sandwich rounds.

3. In a large skillet, heat 2 tablespoons olive oil over medium-high heat. Brush the remaining 2 tablespoons olive oil over the tops of the sandwiches.

4. When the skillet is hot, add each sandwich, unoiled-side down, pressing down with the back of a spatula to grill. Cook 3 to 4 minutes, or until cheese begins to melt, before flipping and pressing down with the back of a spatula. Grill on second side another 3 to 4 minutes, or until golden and cheese is very melted. Serve hot.

Per Serving (1 sandwich): Calories: 598, Total Fat: 56g, Total Carbs: 8g, Net Carbs: 7g, Fiber: 1g, Protein: 16g; Sodium: 950mg

Macros: Fat: 84%, Carbs: 5%, Protein: 11%

Fennel and Cod Chowder with Fried Mushrooms

EGG-FREE, GLUTEN-FREE, NUT-FREE

Serves 4
Prep Time: 20 minutes
Cook Time: 35 minutes

1 cup extra-virgin olive
   oil, divided
1 small head cauliflower,
   core removed and broken
   into florets (about 2 cups)
1 small white onion,
   thinly sliced
1 fennel bulb, white part
   only, trimmed and
   thinly sliced
½ cup dry white wine
   (optional)
2 garlic cloves, minced
1 teaspoon salt
¼ teaspoon freshly ground
   black pepper
4 cups Fish Stock (page 179),
   plus more if needed
1 pound thick cod fillet, cut
   into ¾-inch cubes
4 ounces shiitake
   mushrooms, stems
   trimmed and thinly sliced
   (⅛-inch slices)
¼ cup chopped Italian
   parsley, for garnish
   (optional)
¼ cup plain whole-milk
   Greek yogurt, for garnish
   (optional)

Most chowder recipes use a lot of cream and butter, which, while keto-friendly, makes for a more saturated fat–heavy dish. Keeping true to the flavors and traditions of the Mediterranean Diet, this version uses a flavorful cauliflower purée as its base. Cod is an inexpensive flaky white fish that holds up nicely in this soup, and it can be bought in bulk and kept frozen to have on hand for easy weeknight meals. Fried mushrooms served on top add a nice crispy texture, much like a traditional crouton, but you can omit them if desired.

1. In large stockpot, heat ¼ cup olive oil over medium-high heat. Add the cauliflower florets, onion, and fennel and sauté for 10 to 12 minutes, or until almost tender. Add the white wine (if using), garlic, salt, and pepper and sauté for another 1 to 2 minutes.

2. Add 4 cups fish stock and bring to a boil. Cover, reduce the heat to medium-low, and simmer until vegetables are very tender, another 8 to 10 minutes. Remove from the heat and allow to cool slightly.

3. Using an immersion blender, purée the vegetable mixture, slowly drizzling in ½ cup olive oil, until very smooth and silky, adding additional fish stock if the mixture is too thick.

4. Turn the heat back to medium-high and bring the soup to a low simmer. Add the cod pieces and cook, covered, until the fish is cooked through, about 5 minutes. Remove from the heat and keep covered.

5. In a medium skillet, heat the remaining ¼ cup olive oil over medium-high heat. When very hot, add the mushrooms and fry until crispy. Remove with a slotted spoon and transfer to a plate, reserving the frying oil. Toss the mushrooms with a sprinkle of salt.

6. Serve the chowder hot, topped with fried mushrooms and drizzled with 1 tablespoon reserved frying oil. Garnish with chopped fresh parsley and 1 tablespoon of Greek yogurt (if using).

Substitution Tip: You can substitute celery for the fennel bulb and add 1 to 2 teaspoons fennel seed for flavor.

Per Serving: Calories: 658, Total Fat: 54g, Total Carbs: 15g, Net Carbs: 10g, Fiber: 5g, Protein: 28g; Sodium: 832mg

Macros: Fat: 74%, Carbs: 8%, Protein: 18%

Greek Chicken and "Rice" Soup with Artichokes

DAIRY-FREE, GLUTEN-FREE, NUT-FREE

Serves 4
Prep Time: 10 minutes
Cook Time: 15 minutes

4 cups Chicken Stock
(page 180) or store-bought
chicken stock

2 cups Riced Cauliflower
(page 177), divided

2 large egg yolks

¼ cup freshly squeezed
lemon juice (about
2 lemons)

¾ cup extra-virgin olive
oil, divided

8 ounces cooked chicken,
coarsely chopped

1 (13.75-ounce) can artichoke
hearts, drained and
quartered

¼ cup chopped fresh dill

Avgolemono is a classic sauce similar to hollandaise, made from egg yolks and lemon juice, that is common in Greek, Turkish, Jewish, and Italian cuisines. Here, I add olive oil for richness, and it serves as a flavorful base for a chicken soup that is simple enough to be made midweek. Riced cauliflower adds bulk and a great texture. I like to use store-bought rotisserie chicken for convenience, but feel free to use any left-over cooked or grilled chicken you may have on hand.

1. In a large saucepan, bring the stock to a low boil. Reduce the heat to low and simmer, covered.

2. Transfer 1 cup of the hot stock to a blender or food processor. Add ½ cup raw riced cauliflower, the egg yolks, and lemon juice and purée. While the processor or blender is running, stream in ½ cup olive oil and blend until smooth.

3. Whisking constantly, pour the purée into the simmering stock until well blended together and smooth. Add the chicken and artichokes and simmer until thickened slightly, 8 to 10 minutes. Stir in the dill and remaining 1½ cups riced cauliflower. Serve warm, drizzled with the remaining ¼ cup olive oil.

Per Serving: Calories: 566, Total Fat: 46g, Total Carbs: 14g, Net Carbs: 7g, Fiber: 7g, Protein: 24g; Sodium: 754mg

Macros: Fat: 73%, Carbs: 10%, Protein: 17%

Israeli Salad with Nuts and Seeds

DAIRY-FREE, EGG-FREE, GLUTEN-FREE, VEGAN

Serves 4
Prep Time: 15 minutes

¼ cup pine nuts

¼ cup shelled pistachios

¼ cup coarsely
   chopped walnuts

¼ cup shelled
   pumpkin seeds

¼ cup shelled
   sunflower seeds

2 large English cucumbers,
   unpeeled and
   finely chopped

1 pint cherry tomatoes,
   finely chopped

½ small red onion,
   finely chopped

½ cup finely chopped fresh
   flat-leaf Italian parsley

¼ cup extra-virgin olive oil

2 to 3 tablespoons freshly
   squeezed lemon juice
   (from 1 lemon)

1 teaspoon salt

¼ teaspoon freshly ground
   black pepper

4 cups baby arugula

The most well-known national dish of Israel according to some, this salad is a standard accompaniment to many Israeli meals. This beautifully simple version becomes a meal in itself with protein and healthy fats from a variety of nuts and seeds, which also give it great texture and crunch.

1. In a large dry skillet, toast the pine nuts, pistachios, walnuts, pumpkin seeds, and sunflower seeds over medium-low heat until golden and fragrant, 5 to 6 minutes, being careful not to burn them. Remove from the heat and set aside.

2. In a large bowl, combine the cucumber, tomatoes, red onion, and parsley.

3. In a small bowl, whisk together olive oil, lemon juice, salt, and pepper. Pour over the chopped vegetables and toss to coat.

4. Add the toasted nuts and seeds and arugula and toss with the salad to blend well. Serve at room temperature or chilled.

Per Serving: Calories: 414, Total Fat: 34g, Total Carbs: 17g, Net Carbs: 11g, Fiber: 6g, Protein: 10g; Sodium: 642mg

Macros: Fat: 74%, Carbs: 16%, Protein: 10%

CHAPTER SIX

Vegetarian Sides and Mains

Mediterranean Cauliflower Tabbouleh

DAIRY-FREE, EGG-FREE, GLUTEN-FREE, NUT-FREE, VEGAN

Serves 6

Prep Time: 15 minutes, plus 30 minutes to chill

Cook Time: 5 minutes

6 tablespoons extra-virgin olive oil, divided

4 cups Riced Cauliflower (page 177)

3 garlic cloves, finely minced

1½ teaspoons salt

½ teaspoon freshly ground black pepper

½ large cucumber, peeled, seeded, and chopped

½ cup chopped mint leaves

½ cup chopped Italian parsley

½ cup chopped pitted Kalamata olives

2 tablespoons minced red onion

Juice of 1 lemon (about 2 tablespoons)

2 cups baby arugula or spinach leaves

2 medium avocados, peeled, pitted, and diced

1 cup quartered cherry tomatoes

Tabbouleh is a grain and vegetable side dish common to Mediterranean and Middle Eastern cuisine. Traditionally, it is made with bulgur wheat, but this version substitutes Riced Cauliflower (page 177) to decrease the carbohydrate load without sacrificing the intense flavors from fresh herbs and an olive oil–based dressing. Avocados and arugula are a great addition for unique taste, texture, and awesome nutrition.

1. In a large skillet, heat 2 tablespoons of olive oil over medium-high heat. Add the riced cauliflower, garlic, salt, and pepper and sauté until just tender but not mushy, 3 to 4 minutes. Remove from the heat and place in a large bowl.

2. Add the cucumber, mint, parsley, olives, red onion, lemon juice, and remaining 4 tablespoons olive oil and toss well. Place in the refrigerator, uncovered, and refrigerate for at least 30 minutes, or up to 2 hours.

3. Before serving, add the arugula, avocado, and tomatoes and toss to combine well. Season to taste with salt and pepper and serve cold or at room temperature.

Per Serving: Calories: 235, Total Fat: 21g, Total Carbs: 12g, Net Carbs: 6g, Fiber: 6g, Protein: 4g; Sodium: 623mg

Macros: Fat: 77%, Carbs: 19%, Protein: 4%

Garlicky Broccoli Rabe with Artichokes

DAIRY-FREE, EGG-FREE, GLUTEN-FREE, NUT-FREE, VEGAN

Serves 4
Prep Time: 5 minutes
Cook Time: 10 minutes

2 pounds fresh broccoli rabe
½ cup extra-virgin olive
   oil, divided
3 garlic cloves, finely minced
1 teaspoon salt
1 teaspoon red pepper flakes
1 (13.75-ounce) can artichoke
   hearts, drained and
   quartered
1 tablespoon water
2 tablespoons red
   wine vinegar
Freshly ground black pepper

Broccoli rabe, or rapini, is packed with nutrients, including vitamins C and K, electrolytes calcium and potassium, and dietary fiber, making it a great addition to your plate. You can use regular broccoli instead, but be sure to trim and finely slice the stalk and florets.

1. Trim away any thick lower stems and yellow leaves from the broccoli rabe and discard. Cut into individual florets with a couple inches of thin stem attached.

2. In a large skillet, heat ¼ cup olive oil over medium-high heat. Add the trimmed broccoli, garlic, salt, and red pepper flakes and sauté for 5 minutes, until the broccoli begins to soften. Add the artichoke hearts and sauté for another 2 minutes.

3. Add the water and reduce the heat to low. Cover and simmer until the broccoli stems are tender, 3 to 5 minutes.

4. In a small bowl, whisk together remaining ¼ cup olive oil and the vinegar. Drizzle over the broccoli and artichokes. Season with ground black pepper, if desired.

Per Serving: Calories: 385, Total Fat: 35g, Total Carbs: 18g, Net Carbs: 8g, Fiber: 10g, Protein: 11g; Sodium: 918mg

Macros: Fat: 81%, Carbs: 11%, Protein: 8%

Roasted Eggplant with Mint and Harissa

DAIRY-FREE, EGG-FREE, GLUTEN-FREE, NUT-FREE, VEGAN

Serves 4
Prep Time: 10 minutes
Cook Time: 35 minutes

2 medium eggplants, cut
    into ½-inch cubes
4 tablespoons extra-virgin
    olive oil
1 teaspoon salt
¼ teaspoon freshly ground
    black pepper
1 cup chopped fresh mint
¼ cup Harissa Oil (page 173)
    or store-bought harissa
¼ cup chopped scallions,
    green part only

Full of North African flavors with spice and a touch of sweet from the mint, this vegetable dish is delicious served both warm and chilled. Pair with roasted meat or grilled fish for a complete meal. I like to leave the skin on my eggplant for color and texture, but feel free to peel yours if you prefer. Eggplant will be a bit softer without the skin left on, so reduce the cooking time by 5 to 8 minutes.

1. Preheat the oven to 425°F. Line a baking sheet with parchment paper.

2. In a large bowl, place the eggplant, olive oil, salt, and pepper and toss to coat well.

3. Place the eggplant on the prepared baking sheet, reserving the bowl, and roast for 15 minutes. Remove from the oven and toss the eggplant pieces to flip. Return to the oven and roast until golden and cooked through, another 15 to 20 minutes.

4. When the eggplant is cooked, remove from the oven and return to the large bowl. Add the mint, harissa, and scallions and toss to combine. Serve warm or cover and refrigerate for up to 2 days.

Per Serving: Calories: 300, Total Fat: 28g, Total Carbs: 15g, Net Carbs: 7g, Fiber: 8g, Protein: 3g; Sodium: 589mg

Macros: Fat: 81%, Carbs: 17%, Protein: 2%

Shakshuka

GLUTEN-FREE, NUT-FREE

Serves 4
Prep Time: 10 minutes
Cook Time: 30 minutes

½ cup plus 2 tablespoons
   extra-virgin olive
   oil, divided
½ small yellow onion,
   finely diced
1 red bell pepper, finely diced
1 (14-ounce) can crushed
   tomatoes, with juices
6 ounces frozen spinach,
   thawed and drained
   of excess liquid (about
   1½ cups)
2 garlic cloves, finely minced
1 teaspoon smoked paprika
1 to 2 teaspoons red pepper
   flakes (optional)
1 tablespoon roughly
   chopped capers
6 large eggs
¼ teaspoon freshly ground
   black pepper
¾ cup crumbled feta or
   goat cheese
¼ cup chopped fresh
   flat-leaf parsley or cilantro

Shakshuka, or eggs baked in a spicy tomato-based sauce, is common in both North African and Israeli cuisine and is my favorite version of eggs for dinner. I've made this more of an olive oil-tomato base to keep ratios favorable for a ketogenic approach, and added spinach for an extra boost of nutrition. Adjust the spices to your liking, omitting the red pepper flakes entirely if you prefer things less spicy. Serve with toasted Versatile Sandwich Rounds (page 169) for soaking up the sauce, if desired.

1. Heat broiler on low setting.

2. In a medium, deep oven-safe skillet, heat 2 tablespoons olive oil over medium-high heat. Add the onion and bell pepper and sauté until softened, 5 to 8 minutes.

3. Add the crushed tomatoes and their juices, ½ cup olive oil, spinach, garlic, paprika, red pepper flakes (if using), and capers, stirring to combine. Bring to a boil, then reduce the heat to low, cover, and simmer for 5 minutes.

4. Uncover the pan and gently crack each egg into the simmering sauce, allowing the egg to create a crater in the sauce and being careful to not let eggs touch. Add the pepper, then cover and cook, poaching the eggs until the yolks are just set, eight to 10 minutes. Eight minutes will yield softer yolks, while a longer cooking time will yield firmer yolks.

(Recipe continues)

Shakshuka, continued

5. Uncover the pan and spread the crumbled cheese over top of the eggs and sauce. Transfer to the oven and broil under low heat until the cheese is just slightly browned and bubbly, 3 to 5 minutes. Drizzle with the remaining 2 tablespoons olive oil, top with chopped parsley, and serve warm.

Prep Tip: For an even quicker preparation, substitute 1 jar low-sugar marinara sauce (less than 6 grams) for the onion, bell pepper, crushed tomatoes, and garlic. Skip steps 2 and 3, season the marinara sauce with paprika and red pepper flakes, and bring to a simmer before cracking in the eggs.

Per Serving: Calories: 476, Total Fat: 40g, Total Carbs: 12g, Net Carbs: 7g, Fiber: 5g, Protein: 17g; Sodium: 287mg

Macros: Fat: 76%, Carbs: 10%, Protein: 14%

Crustless Spanakopita

GLUTEN-FREE

Serves 6
Prep Time: 15 minutes
Cook Time: 45 minutes

12 tablespoons extra-virgin
   olive oil, divided
1 small yellow onion, diced
1 (32-ounce) bag frozen
   chopped spinach, thawed,
   fully drained, and patted
   dry (about 4 cups)
4 garlic cloves, minced
½ teaspoon salt
½ teaspoon freshly ground
   black pepper
1 cup whole-milk
   ricotta cheese
4 large eggs
¾ cup crumbled traditional
   feta cheese
¼ cup pine nuts

Spanakopita is a Greek savory pie with a spinach and feta filling inside a flaky phyllo crust. Most versions found in the United States are heavy on the crust and light on the filling. This crustless version is heavy on the spinach and adds in fresh ricotta and eggs for texture and protein. It's a delicious vegetarian meal on its own or you can serve it alongside a light soup for something heartier. Traditional Greek feta is made from sheep's milk and typically found in block form, but a lot of commercial feta in the United States is made from cow's milk and sold crumbled. The flavor of the traditional version is far superior and worth seeking out. Substitute goat cheese if you prefer a less salty flavor.

1. Preheat the oven to 375°F.

2. In a large skillet, heat 4 tablespoons olive oil over medium-high heat. Add the onion and sauté until softened, 6 to 8 minutes.

3. Add the spinach, garlic, salt, and pepper and sauté another 5 minutes. Remove from the heat and allow to cool slightly.

4. In a medium bowl, whisk together the ricotta and eggs. Add to the cooled spinach and stir to combine.

5. Pour 4 tablespoons olive oil in the bottom of a 9-by-13-inch glass baking dish and swirl to coat the bottom and sides. Add the spinach-ricotta mixture and spread into an even layer.

(Recipe continues)

Crustless Spanakopita, continued

6. Bake for 20 minutes or until the mixture begins to set. Remove from the oven and crumble the feta evenly across the top of the spinach. Add the pine nuts and drizzle with the remaining 4 tablespoons olive oil. Return to the oven and bake for an additional 15 to 20 minutes, or until the spinach is fully set and the top is starting to turn golden brown. Allow to cool slightly before cutting to serve.

Leftovers Tip: Pine nuts can be expensive, but I like to buy them in bulk and store them in my freezer for use in various dishes. Sprinkle them on salads for extra crunch or use them to make homemade pesto. The Israeli Salad with Nuts and Seeds (page 83) uses a variety of seeds and nuts, including pine nuts, to create a satisfying crunch and a satiating main course salad.

Per Serving: Calories: 484, Total Fat: 43g, Total Carbs: 10g, Net Carbs: 5g, Fiber: 5g, Protein: 18g; Sodium: 438mg

Macros: Fat: 79%, Carbs: 8%, Protein: 13%

Zucchini Lasagna

EGG-FREE, GLUTEN-FREE, NUT-FREE

Serves 8
Prep Time: 15 minutes
Cook Time: 1 hour

½ cup extra-virgin olive oil, divided

4 to 5 medium zucchini squash

1 teaspoon salt

8 ounces frozen spinach, thawed and well drained (about 1 cup)

2 cups whole-milk ricotta cheese

¼ cup chopped fresh basil or 2 teaspoons dried basil

1 teaspoon garlic powder

½ teaspoon freshly ground black pepper

2 cups shredded fresh whole-milk mozzarella cheese

1¾ cups shredded Parmesan cheese

½ (24-ounce) jar low-sugar marinara sauce (less than 5 grams sugar)

Lasagna is comfort food at its finest. Traditional versions are quite high in carbs and gluten, but this low-carb spin has all the rich creaminess of the old favorite without the pasta hangover! The best part is that this can feed a crowd or make leftovers for the week. I often make two lasagnas at one time, freezing the second for busy weeks ahead. For a non-vegetarian version, you can add cooked grass-fed ground beef to the ricotta and spinach sauce.

1. Preheat the oven to 425°F.

2. Line two baking sheets with parchment paper or aluminum foil and drizzle each with 2 tablespoons olive oil, spreading evenly.

3. Slice the zucchini lengthwise into ¼-inch-thick long slices and place on the prepared baking sheet in a single layer. Sprinkle with ½ teaspoon salt per sheet. Bake until softened, but not mushy, 15 to 18 minutes. Remove from the oven and allow to cool slightly before assembling the lasagna.

4. Reduce the oven temperature to 375°F.

5. While the zucchini cooks, prep the filling. In a large bowl, combine the spinach, ricotta, basil, garlic powder, and pepper. In a small bowl, mix together the mozzarella and Parmesan cheeses. In a medium bowl, combine the marinara sauce and remaining ¼ cup olive oil and stir to fully incorporate the oil into sauce.

(Recipe continues)

Zucchini Lasagna, continued

6. To assemble the lasagna, spoon a third of the marinara sauce mixture into the bottom of a 9-by-13-inch glass baking dish and spread evenly. Place 1 layer of softened zucchini slices to fully cover the sauce, then add a third of the ricotta-spinach mixture and spread evenly on top of the zucchini. Sprinkle a third of the mozzarella-Parmesan mixture on top of the ricotta. Repeat with 2 more cycles of these layers: marinara, zucchini, ricotta-spinach, then cheese blend.

7. Bake until the cheese is bubbly and melted, 30 to 35 minutes. Turn the broiler to low and broil until the top is golden brown, about 5 minutes. Remove from the oven and allow to cool slightly before slicing.

> **Substitution Tip:** You can use eggplant in place of the zucchini, using the same method of cooking ahead before layering in the dish. You could even use a combination of the two for extra variety!

Per Serving: Calories: 521, Total Fat: 41g, Total Carbs: 13g, Net Carbs: 10g, Fiber: 3g, Protein: 25g; Sodium: 712mg

Macros: Fat: 71%, Carbs: 10%, Protein: 19%

Moroccan Vegetable Tagine

DAIRY-FREE, EGG-FREE, GLUTEN-FREE, NUT-FREE, VEGAN

Serves 6
Prep Time: 20 minutes
Cook Time: 1 hour

½ cup extra-virgin olive oil
2 medium yellow
   onions, sliced
6 celery stalks, sliced into
   ¼-inch crescents
6 garlic cloves, minced
1 teaspoon ground cumin
1 teaspoon ginger powder
1 teaspoon salt
1/2 teaspoon paprika
½ teaspoon ground
   cinnamon
¼ teaspoon freshly ground
   black pepper
2 cups vegetable stock
1 medium eggplant, cut into
   1-inch cubes
2 medium zucchini, cut into
   ½-inch-thick semicircles
2 cups cauliflower florets
1 (13.75-ounce) can artichoke
   hearts, drained and
   quartered
1 cup halved and pitted
   green olives
½ cup chopped fresh
   flat-leaf parsley,
   for garnish
½ cup chopped fresh
   cilantro leaves, for garnish
Greek yogurt, for garnish
   (optional)

Tagines, named after the clay pot in which they are cooked, are common in Moroccan cuisine and typically contain meat or poultry. This vegetarian version uses a variety of nutrient-rich vegetables seasoned with rich spices and cooked slowly for intense flavor. I use my Dutch oven for this recipe, but any thick soup pot will do.

1. In a large, thick soup pot or Dutch oven, heat the olive oil over medium-high heat. Add the onion and celery and sauté until softened, 6 to 8 minutes. Add the garlic, cumin, ginger, salt, paprika, cinnamon, and pepper and sauté for another 2 minutes.

2. Add the stock and bring to a boil. Reduce the heat to low and add the eggplant, zucchini, and cauliflower. Simmer on low heat, covered, until the vegetables are tender, 30 to 35 minutes. Add the artichoke hearts and olives, cover, and simmer for another 15 minutes.

3. Serve garnished with parsley, cilantro, and Greek yogurt (if using).

Substitution Tip: You can replace the spice combination used in this recipe with garam masala, an Indian spice blend found in many grocery stores.

Per Serving: Calories: 309, Total Fat: 21g, Total Carbs: 24g, Net Carbs: 15g, Fiber: 9g, Protein: 6g; Sodium: 1167mg

Macros: Fat: 61%, Carbs: 12%, Protein: 27%

Citrus Asparagus with Pistachios

DAIRY-FREE, EGG-FREE, GLUTEN-FREE, VEGAN

Serves 4
Prep Time: 10 minutes
Cook Time: 15 minutes

5 tablespoons extra-virgin
   olive oil, divided
Zest and juice of
   2 clementines or 1 orange
   (about ¼ cup juice and
   1 tablespoon zest)
Zest and juice of 1 lemon
1 tablespoon red
   wine vinegar
1 teaspoon salt, divided
¼ teaspoon freshly ground
   black pepper
½ cup shelled pistachios
1 pound fresh asparagus
1 tablespoon water

Spain is one of Europe's largest asparagus producers and you will see the white and green versions of this delectable vegetable featured in many dishes there. The citrus and pistachios work together nicely to create a light and refreshing side.

1. In a small bowl, whisk together 4 tablespoons olive oil, the clementine and lemon juices and zests, vinegar, ½ teaspoon salt, and pepper. Set aside.

2. In a medium dry skillet, toast the pistachios over medium-high heat until lightly browned, 2 to 3 minutes, being careful not to let them burn. Transfer to a cutting board and coarsely chop. Set aside.

3. Trim the rough ends off the asparagus, usually the last 1 to 2 inches of each spear. In a skillet, heat the remaining 1 tablespoon olive oil over medium-high heat. Add the asparagus and sauté for 2 to 3 minutes. Sprinkle with the remaining ½ teaspoon salt and add the water. Reduce the heat to medium-low, cover, and cook until tender, another 2 to 4 minutes, depending on the thickness of the spears.

4. Transfer the cooked asparagus to a serving dish. Add the pistachios to the dressing and whisk to combine. Pour the dressing over the warm asparagus and toss to coat.

Per Serving: Calories: 284, Total Fat: 24g, Total Carbs: 11g, Net Carbs: 7g, Fiber: 4g, Protein: 6g; Sodium: 594mg

Macros: Fat: 76%, Carbs: 15%, Protein: 9%

Herbed Ricotta-Stuffed Mushrooms

EGG-FREE, GLUTEN-FREE, NUT-FREE

Serves 4
Prep Time: 10 minutes
Cook Time: 30 minutes

6 tablespoons extra-virgin
  olive oil, divided
4 portobello mushroom caps,
  cleaned and gills removed
1 cup whole-milk
  ricotta cheese
⅓ cup chopped fresh herbs
  (such as basil, parsley,
  rosemary, oregano,
  or thyme)
2 garlic cloves, finely minced
½ teaspoon salt
¼ teaspoon freshly ground
  black pepper

Here's another superfast weeknight meal that is still impressive enough to make it look like you spent hours preparing a meal for company—see the substitution tip for an even quicker shortcut. I like using large portobello mushrooms here for a main-course vegetarian meal. You can use smaller porcini or cremini mushrooms for an appetizer, if you prefer. Feel free to substitute a creamy goat cheese such as chèvre for some or all of the ricotta for a different flavor profile.

1. Preheat the oven to 400°F.

2. Line a baking sheet with parchment or foil and drizzle with 2 tablespoons olive oil, spreading evenly. Place the mushroom caps on the baking sheet, gill-side up.

3. In a medium bowl, mix together the ricotta, herbs, 2 tablespoons olive oil, garlic, salt, and pepper. Stuff each mushroom cap with one-quarter of the cheese mixture, pressing down if needed. Drizzle with remaining 2 tablespoons olive oil and bake until golden brown and the mushrooms are soft, 30 to 35 minutes, depending on the size of the mushrooms.

Prep Tip: To make this a super-quick meal, replace the herbs and 2 tablespoons olive oil with 4 ounces jarred pesto.

Per Serving: Calories: 285, Total Fat: 25g, Total Carbs: 8g, Net Carbs: 6g, Fiber: 2g, Protein: 7g; Sodium: 325mg

Macros: Fat: 79%, Carbs: 11%, Protein: 10%

Braised Greens with Olives and Walnuts

DAIRY-FREE, EGG-FREE, GLUTEN-FREE, VEGAN

Serves 4
Prep Time: 5 minutes
Cook Time: 20 minutes

8 cups fresh greens (such as kale, mustard greens, spinach, or chard)
2 to 4 garlic cloves, finely minced
½ cup roughly chopped pitted green or black olives
½ cup roughly chopped shelled walnuts
¼ cup extra-virgin olive oil
2 tablespoons red wine vinegar
1 to 2 teaspoons freshly chopped herbs such as oregano, basil, rosemary, or thyme

This is a great way to use up any leftover greens that are nearing the end of their life. I like the peppery taste of mustard greens along with a milder kale or spinach, but feel free to use anything you have on hand. A softer cabbage such as napa or savoy would work well in this recipe as well. You can add a fried egg or leftover fish or meat for a complete fridge clean-out meal.

1. Remove the tough stems from the greens and chop into bite-size pieces. Place in a large rimmed skillet or pot.

2. Turn the heat to high and add the minced garlic and enough water to just cover the greens. Bring to a boil, reduce the heat to low, and simmer until the greens are wilted and tender and most of the liquid has evaporated, adding more if the greens start to burn. For more tender greens such as spinach, this may only take 5 minutes, while tougher greens such as chard may need up to 20 minutes. Once cooked, remove from the heat and add the chopped olives and walnuts.

3. In a small bowl, whisk together olive oil, vinegar, and herbs. Drizzle over the cooked greens and toss to coat. Serve warm.

Per Serving: Calories: 280, Total Fat: 20g, Total Carbs: 18g, Net Carbs: 13g, Fiber: 5g, Protein: 7g; Sodium: 347mg

Macros: Fat: 65%, Carbs: 25%, Protein: 10%

Pesto Cauliflower Sheet-Pan "Pizza"

EGG-FREE, GLUTEN-FREE

Serves 4
Prep Time: 10 minutes
Cook Time: 35 minutes

1 head cauliflower, trimmed

¼ cup extra-virgin olive oil

1 teaspoon salt

½ teaspoon freshly ground
  black pepper

1 teaspoon garlic powder

4 tablespoons Arugula and
  Walnut Pesto (page 162) or
  store-bought pesto

1 cup shredded whole-milk
  mozzarella or Italian
  cheese blend

½ cup crumbled feta cheese

Many store-bought cauliflower pizza crusts are full of binders and hidden carbs and making your own at home can be a frustrating experience, to say the least. I just haven't been wowed by my own attempts. Here is an alternative that has all the gooey cheesy goodness of pizza, without the crust. It's easy and so addictive even my four-year-old asks for seconds. Feel free to mix up the cheeses with whatever you have on hand. I use jarred pesto in a pinch, but this is even better with a home-made Arugula and Walnut Pesto (page 162).

1. Preheat the oven to 425°F.

2. Remove the stem and bottom leaves from a head of cauliflower and carefully break into large florets—the larger, the better. Thinly slice each floret from top to stem to about ¼-inch thickness.

3. Line a large rimmed baking sheet with aluminum foil and drizzle with the olive oil, spreading the oil around with your fingers to coat the foil. Lay the cauliflower out in a single layer on the oiled sheet. Sprinkle with salt, pepper, and garlic powder.

(Recipe continues)

4. Place in the oven and roast until softened, 15 to 20 minutes. Remove from the oven and spread the pesto evenly over top of the cauliflower. Sprinkle with the shredded cheese and feta, return to the oven, and roast for 10 more minutes, or until the cheese is melted and the cauliflower is soft.

5. Turn the broiler to low and broil until browned and bubbly on top, 3 to 5 minutes. Remove from the oven, allow to cool slightly, and cut into large squares to serve.

Per Serving: Calories: 346, Total Fat: 30g, Total Carbs: 7g, Net Carbs: 5g, Fiber: 2g, Protein: 12g; Sodium: 938mg

Macros: Fat: 78%, Carbs: 8%, Protein: 14%

Greek Stewed Zucchini

EGG-FREE, GLUTEN-FREE, NUT-FREE

Serves 4 to 6
Prep Time: 5 minutes
Cook Time: 40 minutes

¼ cup extra-virgin olive oil

1 small yellow onion, peeled and slivered

4 medium zucchini squash, cut into ½-inch-thick rounds

4 small garlic cloves, minced

1 to 2 teaspoons dried oregano

2 cups chopped tomatoes

½ cup halved and pitted Kalamata olives

¾ cup crumbled feta cheese

¼ cup chopped fresh flat-leaf Italian parsley, for garnish (optional)

Stewing vegetables over low heat in a seasoned liquid produces great flavor and spices up vegetable sides that may be getting tiresome. Feel free to mix up the herbs if you wish; parsley or dill would also be fantastic in this dish. Top with a fried egg for a complete vegetarian meal or serve alongside your favorite roasted or grilled fish or meat.

1. In a large skillet, heat the oil over medium-high heat. Add the slivered onion and sauté until just tender, 6 to 8 minutes. Add the zucchini, garlic, and oregano and sauté another 6 to 8 minutes, or until zucchini is just tender.

2. Add the tomatoes and bring to a boil. Reduce the heat to low and add the olives. Cover and simmer on low heat for 20 minutes, or until the flavors have developed and the zucchini is very tender.

3. Serve warm topped with feta and parsley (if using).

Per Serving: Calories: 272, Total Fat: 20g, Total Carbs: 15g, Net Carbs: 10g, Fiber: 5g, Protein: 8g; Sodium: 488mg

Macros: Fat: 66%, Carbs: 22%, Protein: 12%

Roasted Brussels Sprouts with Tahini-Yogurt Sauce

EGG-FREE, GLUTEN-FREE, NUT-FREE

Serves 4
Prep Time: 10 minutes
Cook Time: 35 minutes

1 pound Brussels sprouts, trimmed and halved lengthwise
6 tablespoons extra-virgin olive oil, divided
1 teaspoon salt, divided
½ teaspoon garlic powder
¼ teaspoon freshly ground black pepper
¼ cup plain whole-milk Greek yogurt
¼ cup tahini
Zest and juice of 1 lemon

Crispy roasted veggies combine with a creamy sauce for a winning combination of flavors and textures. Tahini is a ground sesame seed paste and it can be found in the aisle with the nut butters or ethnic foods in most grocery stores. You can substitute leftover Lemon-Tahini Dressing (page 165) for the yogurt sauce for a dairy-free version.

1. Preheat the oven to 425°F. Line a baking sheet with aluminum foil or parchment paper and set aside.

2. Place the Brussels sprouts in a large bowl. Drizzle with 4 tablespoons olive oil, ½ teaspoon salt, the garlic powder, and pepper and toss well to coat.

3. Place the Brussels sprouts in a single layer on the baking sheet, reserving the bowl, and roast for 20 minutes. Remove from the oven and give the sprouts a toss to flip. Return to the oven and continue to roast until browned and crispy, another 10 to 15 minutes. Remove from the oven and return to the reserved bowl.

4. In a small bowl, whisk together the yogurt, tahini, lemon zest and juice, remaining 2 tablespoons olive oil, and remaining ½ teaspoon salt. Drizzle over the roasted sprouts and toss to coat. Serve warm.

Per Serving: Calories: 358, Total Fat: 30g, Total Carbs: 15g, Net Carbs: 9g, Fiber: 6g, Protein: 7g; Sodium: 636mg

Macros: Fat: 75%, Carbs: 17%, Protein: 8%

Asparagus Frittata

DAIRY-FREE, GLUTEN-FREE, NUT-FREE

Serves 4
Prep Time: 10 minutes
Cook Time: 20 minutes

8 tablespoons extra-virgin
   olive oil, divided
¼ cup finely chopped white
   onion (about
   ½ small onion)
1 pound medium-thin
   asparagus, rough stalks
   trimmed, cut into
   1-inch pieces
2 medium garlic
   cloves, minced
6 large eggs
2 tablespoons
   vegetable broth
1 teaspoon salt
½ teaspoon freshly ground
   black pepper
4 tablespoons Zesty Orange
   or Roasted Garlic Aioli
   (page 166–167), for serving
½ cup chopped herbs (basil,
   parsley, or mint), for
   garnish (optional)

You'll be hard pressed to find a restaurant or tapas bar in Spain that doesn't have some version of this on the menu. So common is the tortilla that many fast-food sandwich, or *bocadillo*, joints serve nothing but *bocadillo de tortilla*, slathered with mayo and sometimes topped with tomato. Not at all what we think of in the United States as a Mexican tortilla, the Spanish version is an egg and potato pancake that, when made without the potato, becomes a wonderfully keto-friendly Mediterranean go-to.

1. In an 8- to 10-inch skillet, heat 4 tablespoons olive oil over medium heat. Add the onion and sauté for 3 to 4 minutes, until the onion begins to soften.

2. Add the asparagus and garlic and cook until asparagus is tender, 5 to 6 minutes. Transfer the cooked vegetables to a bowl and let cool. Wipe any cooked food from the skillet, but do not wash.

3. In a medium bowl, whisk together the eggs, vegetable broth, salt, and pepper. Add the cooled asparagus and mix until well combined.

4. In the same skillet, heat 2 tablespoons of olive oil over medium-high heat. Pour the egg mixture into the skillet and reduce the heat to medium-low. Let the eggs cook undisturbed for 2 to 3 minutes, or until the bottom begins to set.

(Recipe continues)

....

5. Run a thin spatula around the edge to allow the uncooked eggs to move towards the bottom of the pan. Cook, continuously moving the uncooked egg mixture until the top is a little wet but not liquid, 3 to 5 minutes.

6. Run the thin spatula under the cooking tortilla to make sure that no part of the bottom is stuck to the skillet. Place a large flat plate or cutting board on top of the skillet and quickly invert the tortilla to the flat surface.

7. Add the remaining 2 tablespoons olive oil to the skillet and carefully slide the tortilla back into the pan, uncooked-side down. Cook over low heat until cooked through, another 2 to 3 minutes.

8. Transfer back to the plate or cutting board. Allow to rest for 5 minutes before slicing.

9. Serve warm or at room temperature with aioli and chopped fresh herbs (if using).

Per Serving: Calories: 444, Total Fat: 40g, Total Carbs: 9g, Net Carbs: 6g, Fiber: 3g, Protein: 12g; Sodium: 795mg

Macros: Fat: 80%, Carbs: 9%, Protein: 11%

CHAPTER SEVEN

Fish and Seafood

Garlicky Shrimp with Mushrooms

DAIRY-FREE, EGG-FREE, GLUTEN-FREE, NUT-FREE

Serves 4
Prep Time: 10 minutes
Cook Time: 15 minutes

1 pound peeled and deveined
   fresh shrimp
1 teaspoon salt
1 cup extra-virgin olive oil
8 large garlic cloves,
   thinly sliced
4 ounces sliced mushrooms
   (shiitake, baby bella,
   or button)
½ teaspoon red
   pepper flakes
¼ cup chopped fresh
   flat-leaf Italian parsley
Zucchini Noodles (page 176)
   or Riced Cauliflower
   (page 177), for serving

Gambas al Ajillo, as this dish is called in Spanish, is a common tapa found in restaurants throughout Madrid. Here, it is elevated to main course status with sautéed mushrooms and served over Zucchini Noodles (page 176) or cauliflower fried rice to soak up all of the garlicky olive oil goodness.

1. Rinse the shrimp and pat dry. Place in a small bowl and sprinkle with the salt.

2. In a large rimmed, thick skillet, heat the olive oil over medium-low heat. Add the garlic and heat until very fragrant, 3 to 4 minutes, reducing the heat if the garlic starts to burn.

3. Add the mushrooms and sauté for 5 minutes, until softened. Add the shrimp and red pepper flakes and sauté until the shrimp begins to turn pink, another 3 to 4 minutes.

4. Remove from the heat and stir in the parsley. Serve over Zucchini Noodles (page 176) or Riced Cauliflower (page 177).

Leftovers Tip: Serve the shrimp chilled over mixed greens for an easy lunch. Whisk 1 to 2 tablespoons red wine vinegar or lemon juice into the garlic oil for an easy vinaigrette.

Per Serving: Calories: 620, Total Fat: 56g, Total Carbs: 4g, Net Carbs: 4g, Fiber: 0g, Protein: 24g; Sodium: 736mg

Macros: Fat: 81% Carbs: 4% Protein: 15%

Swordfish in Tarragon-Citrus Butter

EGG-FREE, GLUTEN-FREE, NUT-FREE

Serves 4
Prep Time: 5 minutes
Cook Time: 20 minutes

1 pound swordfish steaks, cut
　into 2-inch pieces
1 teaspoon salt
¼ teaspoon freshly ground
　black pepper
¼ cup extra-virgin olive oil,
　plus 2 tablespoons, divided
2 tablespoons
　unsalted butter
Zest and juice of
　2 clementines
Zest and juice of 1 lemon
2 tablespoons chopped fresh
　tarragon
Sautéed greens, Riced
　Cauliflower (page 177), or
　Zucchini Noodles
　(page 176), for serving

This is my Ketogenic Mediterranean adaptation of a meal I had several years ago with scallops in a rich, buttery sauce served over creamy polenta. When not overcooked, swordfish has a buttery consistency similar to that of scallops, so I find it to be a less-expensive option for this dish, but feel free to use fresh sea scallops if you feel like splurging.

1. In a bowl, toss the swordfish with salt and pepper.

2. In a large skillet, heat ¼ cup olive oil over medium-high heat. Add the swordfish chunks to the hot oil and sear on all sides, 2 to 3 minutes per side, until they are lightly golden brown. Using a slotted spoon, remove the fish from the pan and keep warm.

3. Add the remaining 2 tablespoons olive oil and butter to the oil already in the pan and return the heat to medium-low. Once the butter has melted, whisk in the clementine and lemon zests and juices, along with the tarragon. Season with salt. Return the fish pieces to the pan and toss to coat in the butter sauce. Serve the fish drizzled with sauce over sautéed greens, Riced Cauliflower (page 177), or Zucchini Noodles (page 176).

Per Serving: Calories: 379, Total Fat: 31g, Total Carbs: 3g, Net Carbs: 3g, Fiber: 0g, Protein: 23g; Sodium: 724mg

Macros: Fat: 71%, Carbs: 3%, Protein: 26%

Escabeche

DAIRY-FREE, EGG-FREE, GLUTEN-FREE, NUT-FREE

Serves 4
Prep Time: 10 minutes
Cook Time: 20 minutes,
plus 15 minutes to rest

1 pound wild-caught Spanish
  mackerel fillets, cut into
  four pieces
1 teaspoon salt
½ teaspoon freshly ground
  black pepper
8 tablespoons extra-virgin
  olive oil, divided
1 bunch asparagus, trimmed
  and cut into 2-inch pieces
1 (13.75-ounce) can artichoke
  hearts, drained and
  quartered
4 large garlic cloves, peeled
  and crushed
2 bay leaves
¼ cup red wine vinegar
½ teaspoon smoked paprika

Escabeche is a generic term for a wide variety of Mediterranean dishes in which fish or meat is marinated and cooked in a mixture of briny vegetables. It can be served warm or cold, and variations are commonly found canned and available at gas stations and convenience stores throughout Europe. I subsisted on variations of these meals-in-a-can on many a road trip while living in Spain and they are absolutely delicious!

1. Sprinkle the fillets with salt and pepper and let sit at room temperature for 5 minutes.

2. In a large skillet, heat 2 tablespoons olive oil over medium-high heat. Add the fish, skin-side up, and cook 5 minutes. Flip and cook 5 minutes on the other side, until browned and cooked through. Transfer to a serving dish, pour the cooking oil over the fish, and cover to keep warm.

3. Heat the remaining 6 tablespoons olive oil in the same skillet over medium heat. Add the asparagus, artichokes, garlic, and bay leaves and sauté until the vegetables are tender, 6 to 8 minutes.

Escabeche, continued

4. Using a slotted spoon, top the fish with the cooked vegetables, reserving the oil in the skillet. Add the vinegar and paprika to the oil and whisk to combine well. Pour the vinaigrette over the fish and vegetables and let sit at room temperature for at least 15 minutes, or marinate in the refrigerator up to 24 hours for a deeper flavor. Remove the bay leaf before serving.

Substitution Tip: You can use mackerel fillets canned in oil and skip the cooking step for convenience, or substitute cod or halibut and follow the recipe as-is.

Per Serving: Calories: 578, Total Fat: 50g, Total Carbs: 13g, Net Carbs: 8g, Fiber: 5g, Protein: 26g; Sodium: 946mg

Macros: Fat: 76%, Carbs: 6%, Protein: 18%

Tuna Slow-Cooked in Olive Oil

DAIRY-FREE, EGG-FREE, GLUTEN-FREE, NUT-FREE

Serves 4
Prep Time: 5 minutes
Cook Time: 45 minutes

1 cup extra-virgin olive oil, plus more if needed
4 (3- to 4-inch) sprigs fresh rosemary
8 (3- to 4-inch) sprigs fresh thyme
2 large garlic cloves, thinly sliced
2 (2-inch) strips lemon zest
1 teaspoon salt
½ teaspoon freshly ground black pepper
1 pound fresh tuna steaks (about 1 inch thick)

This is the tuna that is used for traditional tuna Niçoise salad. While a bit more labor intensive, after tasting it, you may never buy canned tuna again! In this flavorful slow-cooked dish, tuna is submerged in olive oil and cooked at low heat for maximum flavor and amazing texture. Another steaky fish, such as swordfish or king mackerel, could stand in for the tuna if you prefer.

1. Select a thick pot just large enough to fit the tuna in a single layer on the bottom. The larger the pot, the more olive oil you will need to use. Combine the olive oil, rosemary, thyme, garlic, lemon zest, salt, and pepper over medium-low heat and cook until warm and fragrant, 20 to 25 minutes, lowering the heat if it begins to smoke.

2. Remove from the heat and allow to cool for 25 to 30 minutes, until warm but not hot.

3. Add the tuna to the bottom of the pan, adding additional oil if needed so that tuna is fully submerged, and return to medium-low heat. Cook for 5 to 10 minutes, or until the oil heats back up and is warm and fragrant but not smoking. Lower the heat if it gets too hot.

4. Remove the pot from the heat and let the tuna cook in warm oil 4 to 5 minutes, to your desired level of doneness. For a tuna that is rare in the center, cook for 2 to 3 minutes.

Tuna Slow-Cooked in Olive Oil, continued

5.   Remove from the oil and serve warm, drizzling 2 to 3 tablespoons seasoned oil over the tuna.

6.   To store for later use, remove the tuna from the oil and place in a container with a lid. Allow tuna and oil to cool separately. When both have cooled, remove the herb stems with a slotted spoon and pour the cooking oil over the tuna. Cover and store in the refrigerator for up to 1 week. Bring to room temperature to allow the oil to liquify before serving.

Per Serving: Calories: 363, Total Fat: 28g, Total Carbs: 1g, Net Carbs: 1g, Fiber: 0g, Protein: 27g; Sodium: 624mg

Macros: Fat: 68%, Carbs: 1%, Protein: 31%

Shrimp Ceviche Salad

DAIRY-FREE, EGG-FREE, GLUTEN-FREE, NUT-FREE

Serves 4

Prep Time: 15 minutes, plus 2 hours to marinate

1 pound fresh shrimp, peeled and deveined

1 small red or yellow bell pepper, cut into ½-inch chunks

½ English cucumber, peeled and cut into ½-inch chunks

½ small red onion, cut into thin slivers

¼ cup chopped fresh cilantro or flat-leaf Italian parsley

⅓ cup freshly squeezed lime juice

2 tablespoons freshly squeezed lemon juice

2 tablespoons freshly squeezed clementine juice or orange juice

½ cup extra-virgin olive oil

1 teaspoon salt

½ teaspoon freshly ground black pepper

2 ripe avocados, peeled, pitted, and cut into ½-inch chunks

Ceviche is a wonderfully light and refreshing seafood preparation that uses no heat at all! Rather, the seafood "cooks" in citrus juices for hours in the refrigerator. You want to make sure to not let it sit too long or the shrimp will get tough and chewy. By cutting the shrimp in half lengthwise, you can reduce the "cooking" time to just around 2 hours. Serve with Seedy Crackers (page 181) atop a bed of mixed greens, or on its own for a light and refreshing meal.

1. Cut the shrimp in half lengthwise. In a large glass bowl, combine the shrimp, bell pepper, cucumber, onion, and cilantro.

2. In a small bowl, whisk together the lime, lemon, and clementine juices, olive oil, salt, and pepper. Pour the mixture over the shrimp and veggies and toss to coat. Cover and refrigerate for at least 2 hours, or up to 8 hours. Give the mixture a toss every 30 minutes for the first 2 hours to make sure all the shrimp "cook" in the juices.

3. Add the cut avocado just before serving and toss to combine.

Per Serving: Calories: 497, Total Fat: 40g, Total Carbs: 14g, Net Carbs: 8g, Fiber: 6g, Protein: 25g; Sodium: 756mg

Macros: Fat: 69%, Carbs: 10%, Protein: 21%

Greek Stuffed Squid

EGG-FREE, GLUTEN-FREE, NUT-FREE

Serves 4
Prep Time: 15 minutes
Cook Time: 30 minutes

8 ounces frozen spinach,
   thawed and drained
   (about 1½ cup)
4 ounces crumbled
   goat cheese
½ cup chopped pitted
   olives (I like Kalamata in
   this recipe)
½ cup extra-virgin olive
   oil, divided
¼ cup chopped sun-dried
   tomatoes
¼ cup chopped fresh
   flat-leaf Italian parsley
2 garlic cloves, finely minced
¼ teaspoon freshly ground
   black pepper
2 pounds baby
   squid, cleaned and
   tentacles removed

If you think squid can only be served breaded and fried as an appetizer, you are wrong! Seafood dishes containing squid and octopus are frequently found on restaurant menus across the Mediterranean. I love how versatile this protein is—with its mild flavor, it really will take on the flavors of whatever you cook it with. Here, baby squid is stuffed with a flavorful goat cheese blend and baked to perfection. It's a low-carb Greek spin on Italian stuffed manicotti.

1.   Preheat the oven to 350°F.

2.   In a medium bowl, combine the spinach, goat cheese, olives, ¼ cup olive oil, sun-dried tomatoes, parsley, garlic, and pepper.

3.   Pour 2 tablespoons olive oil in the bottom of an 8-inch square baking dish and spread to coat the bottom.

4.   Stuff each cleaned squid with 2 to 3 tablespoons of the cheese mixture, depending on the size of squid, and place in the prepared baking dish.

(Recipe continues)

5. Drizzle the tops with the remaining 2 tablespoons olive oil and bake until the squid are cooked through, 25 to 30 minutes. Remove from the oven and allow to cool 5 to 10 minutes before serving.

> **Substitution Tip:** This recipe calls for baby squid, which are cylindrical in shape and easy to stuff, much like a large pasta shell, but I have also made this using calamari steaks, placing filling in the center and rolling like an enchilada before placing in the baking dish. Since the steaks are thicker, you will need to increase the cooking time by 10 to 15 minutes.

Per Serving: Calories: 469, Total Fat: 37g, Total Carbs: 10g, Net Carbs: 7g, Fiber: 3g, Protein: 24g; Sodium: 576mg

Macros: Fat: 71% Carbs: 9% Protein: 20%

Seafood Fideo

EGG-FREE, GLUTEN-FREE, NUT-FREE

Serves 6 to 8
Prep Time: 15 minutes
Cook Time: 20 minutes

2 tablespoons extra-virgin
olive oil, plus
½ cup, divided

6 cups Zucchini Noodles
(page 176), roughly
chopped (2 to 3 medium
zucchini)

1 pound shrimp,
peeled, deveined and
roughly chopped

6 to 8 ounces canned
chopped clams, drained
(about 3 to 4 ounces
drained)

4 ounces crabmeat

½ cup crumbled
goat cheese

½ cup crumbled feta cheese

1 (28-ounce) can chopped
tomatoes, with their juices

1 teaspoon salt

1 teaspoon garlic powder

½ teaspoon smoked paprika

½ cup shredded
Parmesan cheese

¼ cup chopped fresh
flat-leaf Italian parsley,
for garnish

Baked pasta dishes are common in northern Spain, while rice paellas are more common in central and southern Spain. Thin, vermicelli-like noodles called *fideos* are usually fried, added to a vegetable and protein base, then baked or cooked over an open fire. Here, I substitute zucchini fideos for the traditional wheat-based version and create more of a creamy tomato base with the addition of goat and feta cheeses.

1. Preheat the oven to 375°F.

2. Pour 2 tablespoons olive oil in the bottom of a 9-by-13-inch baking dish and swirl to coat the bottom.

3. In a large bowl, combine the zucchini noodles, shrimp, clams, and crabmeat.

4. In another bowl, combine the goat cheese, feta, and ¼ cup olive oil and stir to combine well. Add the canned tomatoes and their juices, salt, garlic powder, and paprika and combine well. Add the mixture to the zucchini and seafood mixture and stir to combine.

5. Pour the mixture into the prepared baking dish, spreading evenly. Spread shredded Parmesan over top and drizzle with the remaining ¼ cup olive oil. Bake until bubbly, 20 to 25 minutes. Serve warm, garnished with chopped parsley.

Per Serving: Calories: 434, Total Fat: 31g, Total Carbs: 12g, Net Carbs: 9g, Fiber: 3g, Protein: 29g; Sodium: 712mg

Macros: Fat: 63%, Carbs: 10%, Protein: 27%

Cod with Parsley Pistou

DAIRY-FREE, EGG-FREE, GLUTEN-FREE, NUT-FREE

Serves 4
Prep Time: 15 minutes
Cook Time: 10 minutes

1 cup packed roughly
   chopped fresh flat-leaf
   Italian parsley
1 to 2 small garlic
   cloves, minced
Zest and juice of 1 lemon
1 teaspoon salt
½ teaspoon freshly ground
   black pepper
1 cup extra-virgin olive
   oil, divided
1 pound cod fillets, cut into
   4 equal-sized pieces

Most Americans know of the herby, garlicky, oil-based condiment for meat, fish, and pastas as pesto, but every country has its own version of this staple. In Latin American countries, they have chimichurri, and in France, they have pistou. The method is mostly the same and really any herb can be used, but I love the distinct flavor of parsley.

1. In a food processer, combine the parsley, garlic, lemon zest and juice, salt, and pepper. Pulse to chop well.

2. While the food processor is running, slowly stream in ¾ cup olive oil until well combined. Set aside.

3. In a large skillet, heat the remaining ¼ cup olive oil over medium-high heat. Add the cod fillets, cover, and cook 4 to 5 minutes on each side, or until cooked through. Thicker fillets may require a bit more cooking time. Remove from the heat and keep warm.

4. Add the pistou to the skillet and heat over medium-low heat. Return the cooked fish to the skillet, flipping to coat in the sauce. Serve warm, covered with pistou.

Leftovers Tip: You can double the ingredients for the parsley pistou and keep this versatile sauce on hand for flavoring eggs, salads, and other grilled meats or seafoods.

Per Serving: Calories: 581, Total Fat: 55g, Total Carbs: 3g, Net Carbs: 2g, Fiber: 1g, Protein: 21g; Sodium: 652mg

Macros: Fat: 84%, Carbs: 1%, Protein: 15%

Rosemary-Lemon Snapper Baked in Parchment

DAIRY-FREE, EGG-FREE, GLUTEN-FREE, NUT-FREE

Serves 4
Prep Time: 15 minutes
Cook Time: 15 minutes

1¼ pounds fresh red
   snapper fillet, cut into two
   equal pieces
2 lemons, thinly sliced
6 to 8 sprigs fresh rosemary,
   stems removed or 1 to
   2 tablespoons dried
   rosemary
½ cup extra-virgin olive oil
6 garlic cloves, thinly sliced
1 teaspoon salt
½ teaspoon freshly ground
   black pepper

Baking fish with a variety of fresh herbs and oil in little parchment pouches is a common cooking method in Italy. In summer months, I've made these in foil pouches on the grill alongside some fresh veggies.

1. Preheat the oven to 425°F.

2. Place two large sheets of parchment (about twice the size of each piece of fish) on the counter. Place 1 piece of fish in the center of each sheet.

3. Top the fish pieces with lemon slices and rosemary leaves.

4. In a small bowl, combine the olive oil, garlic, salt, and pepper. Drizzle the oil over each piece of fish.

5. Top each piece of fish with a second large sheet of parchment and starting on a long side, fold the paper up to about 1 inch from the fish. Repeat on the remaining sides, going in a clockwise direction. Fold in each corner once to secure.

6. Place both parchment pouches on a baking sheet and bake until the fish is cooked through, 10 to 12 minutes.

Per Serving: Calories: 390, Total Fat: 29g, Total Carbs: 3g, Net Carbs: 3g, Fiber: 0g, Protein: 29g; Sodium: 674mg

Macros: Fat: 66%, Carbs: 2%, Protein: 32%

Shrimp in Creamy Pesto over Zoodles

EGG-FREE, GLUTEN-FREE

Serves 4
Prep Time: 10 minutes
Cook Time: 10 minutes

1 pound peeled and
 deveined fresh shrimp
Salt
Freshly ground black pepper
2 tablespoons extra-virgin
 olive oil
½ small onion, slivered
8 ounces store-bought
 jarred pesto
¾ cup crumbled goat or
 feta cheese, plus more
 for serving
6 cups Zucchini Noodles
 (page 176; from about 2
 large zucchini), for serving
¼ cup chopped flat-leaf
 Italian parsley, for garnish

This easy weeknight recipe uses jarred pesto for convenience, but it is also delicious with the Arugula and Walnut Pesto (page 162) if you have that on hand. You can make this with chicken thighs as well, browning the thighs with the onions. Remove them before bringing the pesto and cheese to a simmer, then return them to the sauce until cooked through, about 20 minutes.

1. In a bowl, season the shrimp with salt and pepper and set aside.

2. In a large skillet, heat the olive oil over medium-high heat. Sauté the onion until just golden, 5 to 6 minutes.

3. Reduce the heat to low and add the pesto and cheese, whisking to combine and melt the cheese. Bring to a low simmer and add the shrimp. Reduce the heat back to low and cover. Cook until the shrimp is cooked through and pink, another 3 to 4 minutes.

4. Serve warm over Zucchini Noodles (page 176), garnishing with chopped parsley and additional crumbled cheese, if desired.

Per Serving: Calories: 491, Total Fat: 35g, Total Carbs: 15g, Net Carbs: 11g, Fiber: 4g, Protein: 29g; Sodium: 870mg

Macros: Fat: 65% Carbs: 10% Protein: 25%

Salmon with Tarragon-Dijon Sauce

DAIRY-FREE, GLUTEN-FREE, NUT-FREE

Serves 4
Prep Time: 5 minutes
Cook Time: 15 minutes,
plus 10 minutes to rest

1 ¼ pounds salmon fillet
   (skin on or removed),
   cut into 4 equal pieces
¼ cup avocado oil
   mayonnaise
¼ cup Dijon or
   stone-ground mustard
Zest and juice of ½ lemon
2 tablespoons chopped
   fresh tarragon or 1 to
   2 teaspoons dried
   tarragon
½ teaspoon salt
¼ teaspoon freshly ground
   black pepper
4 tablespoons extra-virgin
   olive oil, for serving

Many people want to include more salmon into their diet for its wonderful health benefits but are intimidated when it comes to preparing it. There certainly is nothing worse than dried-out, overcooked salmon! The light and creamy sauce in this recipe tops each cut of salmon to help it retain moisture, while baking the fish until just undercooked and allowing it to finish out of the oven keeps it from getting overcooked.

1.   Preheat the oven to 425°F. Line a baking sheet with parchment paper.

2.   Place the salmon pieces, skin-side down, on a baking sheet.

3.   In a small bowl, whisk together the mayonnaise, mustard, lemon zest and juice, tarragon, salt, and pepper. Top the salmon evenly with the sauce mixture.

4.   Bake until slightly browned on top and slightly translucent in the center, 10 to 12 minutes, depending on the thickness of the salmon. Remove from the oven and leave on the baking sheet for 10 minutes. Drizzle each fillet with 1 tablespoon olive oil before serving.

Per Serving: Calories: 387, Total Fat: 28g, Total Carbs: 4g, Net Carbs: 3g, Fiber: 1g, Protein: 29g; Sodium: 633mg

Macros: Fat: 64%, Carbs: 5%, Protein: 31%

Nut-Crusted Baked Fish

DAIRY-FREE, EGG-FREE, GLUTEN-FREE

Serves 4
Prep Time: 10 minutes
Cook Time: 20 minutes

½ cup extra-virgin olive
   oil, divided
1 pound flaky white fish
   (such as cod, haddock, or
   halibut), skin removed
½ cup shelled finely
   chopped pistachios
½ cup ground flaxseed
Zest and juice of
   1 lemon, divided
1 teaspoon ground cumin
1 teaspoon ground allspice
½ teaspoon salt (use
   1 teaspoon if pistachios
   are unsalted)
¼ teaspoon freshly ground
   black pepper

A common Lebanese recipe is lean fish baked with a rich tahini-based sauce. This variation creates a crispy fish with those same nutty flavors by coating the fish in nuts rather than using a sauce. You'll want to use a light, flaky fish—such as cod, haddock, or halibut—for the best texture. I like using finely chopped pistachios here, as they have a slightly sweet taste that mixes well with the savory spices, but any nut will do.

1. Preheat the oven to 400°F.

2. Line a baking sheet with parchment paper or aluminum foil and drizzle 2 tablespoons olive oil over the sheet, spreading to evenly coat the bottom.

3. Cut the fish into 4 equal pieces and place on the prepared baking sheet.

4. In a small bowl, combine the pistachios, flaxseed, lemon zest, cumin, allspice, salt, and pepper. Drizzle in ¼ cup olive oil and stir well.

5. Divide the nut mixture evenly atop the fish pieces. Drizzle the lemon juice and remaining 2 tablespoons oil over the fish and bake until cooked through, 15 to 20 minutes, depending on the thickness of the fish.

Per Serving: Calories: 509, Total Fat: 41g, Total Carbs: 9g, Net Carbs: 3g, Fiber: 6g, Protein: 26g; Sodium: 331mg

Macros: Fat: 72% Carbs: 8% Protein: 20%

Salmon Cakes with Avocado

DAIRY-FREE, GLUTEN-FREE

Serves 4
Prep Time: 15 minutes,
plus 15 minutes to rest
Cook Time: 15 minutes

1 (14.5-ounce) can red
   salmon or 1 pound
   wild-caught salmon filet,
   skin removed
½ cup minced red onion
1 large egg
2 tablespoons avocado oil
   mayonnaise, plus more
   for serving
1 very ripe avocado, pitted,
   peeled, and mashed
½ cup almond flour
1 to 2 teaspoons dried dill
1 teaspoon garlic powder
1 teaspoon salt
½ teaspoon paprika
½ teaspoon freshly ground
   black pepper
Zest and juice of 1 lemon
¼ cup extra-virgin olive oil
Roasted Garlic Aioli
   (page 167), for serving

Here's a fun way to get even more salmon goodness in your diet. You can use fresh skinless fillets, but canned salmon (which is less expensive than fresh) typically contains more tiny bones that are softened through the canning process and not detectable in the final product—this adds a heavy dose of calcium! Just make sure to look for wild-caught red salmon, preferably sockeye. Unlike many seafood dishes, these are freezer friendly, making cooking a big batch for use in later meals a huge plus.

1. Remove the spine, large bones, and pieces of skin from the salmon. Place the salmon and red onion in a large bowl and using a fork, break up any lumps.

2. Add the egg, mayonnaise, and avocado and combine well.

3. In a small bowl, whisk together the almond flour, dill, garlic powder, salt, paprika, and pepper.

4. Add the dry ingredients and lemon zest and juice to the salmon and combine well.

5. Form into 8 small patties, about 2 inches in diameter and place on a plate. Let rest for 15 minutes.

(Recipe continues)

6. In a large cast iron skillet, heat the olive oil over medium heat. Fry the patties until browned, 2 to 3 minutes per side. Cover the skillet, reduce heat to low, and cook another 6 to 8 minutes, or until the cakes are set in the center. Remove from the skillet and serve warm with additional mayonnaise or Roasted Garlic Aioli (page 167).

Leftovers Tip: Unlike many other seafood dishes, these reheat really nicely and can be stored in the fridge or freezer for using midweek atop a salad, crumbled in scrambled eggs, or for a quick higher-protein snack.

Per Serving: Calories: 343, Total Fat: 26g, Total Carbs: 5g, Net Carbs: 4g, Fiber: 1g, Protein: 23g; Sodium: 696mg

Macros: Fat: 66%, Carbs: 6%, Protein: 28%

Salt-and-Pepper Scallops and Calamari

DAIRY-FREE, EGG-FREE, GLUTEN-FREE, NUT-FREE

Serves 4

Prep Time: 5 minutes, plus 15 minutes to rest

Cook Time: 10 minutes

8 ounces calamari steaks, cut into ½-inch-thick strips or rings

8 ounces sea scallops

1½ teaspoons salt, divided

1 teaspoon freshly ground black pepper

1 teaspoon garlic powder

⅓ cup extra-virgin olive oil

2 tablespoons butter

I love how simple this dish is, yet it still feels like a treat. This is so family friendly that my four-year-old has requested that we have these every night! You can substitute shrimp for the calamari steaks if you have trouble finding them, or use a light flaky fish such as cod or halibut.

1. Place the calamari and scallops on several layers of paper towels and pat dry. Sprinkle with 1 teaspoon salt and allow to sit for 15 minutes at room temperature. Pat dry with additional paper towels. Sprinkle with pepper and garlic powder.

2. In a deep medium skillet, heat the olive oil and butter over medium-high heat. When the oil is hot but not smoking, add the scallops and calamari in a single layer to the skillet and sprinkle with the remaining ½ teaspoon salt. Cook 2 to 4 minutes on each side, depending on the size of the scallops, until just golden but still slightly opaque in center.

3. Using a slotted spoon, remove from the skillet and transfer to a serving platter. Allow the cooking oil to cool slightly and drizzle over the seafood before serving.

Per Serving: Calories: 309, Total Fat: 25g, Total Carbs: 3g, Net Carbs: 3g, Fiber: 0g, Protein: 18g; Sodium: 928mg

Macros: Fat: 71%, Carbs: 4%, Protein: 25%

CHAPTER EIGHT

Meat and Poultry

Braised Short Ribs with Red Wine

DAIRY-FREE, EGG-FREE, GLUTEN-FREE, NUT-FREE

Serves 4
Prep Time: 10 minutes
Cook Time: 1½ to 2 hours

1½ pounds boneless beef
   short ribs (if using bone-in,
   use 3½ pounds)
1 teaspoon salt
½ teaspoon freshly ground
   black pepper
½ teaspoon garlic powder
¼ cup extra-virgin olive oil
1 cup dry red wine (such
   as cabernet sauvignon
   or merlot)
2 to 3 cups beef
   broth, divided
4 sprigs rosemary

This is a wonderfully rich luxury meal. While the Mediterranean Diet focuses on seafood and leaner proteins, quality red meat makes for a heartier splurge once or twice a month. Many braised meat recipes call for using all wine, but by using a blend of beef broth with just enough wine for flavor, this recipe cuts back on the carbs and sugar. Serve these decadent short ribs with mashed cauliflower and sautéed green vegetables.

1. Preheat the oven to 350°F.

2. Season the short ribs with salt, pepper, and garlic powder. Let sit for 10 minutes.

3. In a Dutch oven or oven-safe deep skillet, heat the olive oil over medium-high heat.

4. When the oil is very hot, add the short ribs and brown until dark in color, 2 to 3 minutes per side. Remove the meat from the oil and keep warm.

5. Add the red wine and 2 cups beef broth to the Dutch oven, whisk together, and bring to a boil. Reduce the heat to low and simmer until the liquid is reduced to about 2 cups, about 10 minutes.

(Recipe continues)

6.   Return the short ribs to the liquid, which should come about halfway up the meat, adding up to 1 cup of remaining broth if needed. Cover and braise until the meat is very tender, about 1½ to 2 hours.

7.   Remove from the oven and let sit, covered, for 10 minutes before serving. Serve warm, drizzled with cooking liquid.

Cooking Tip: Don't skimp on the cooking time. This is a treat meal meant to be slow-cooked and slowly enjoyed! Searing the meat first locks in flavor while slow-cooking or braising in the liquid creates an unmatched tenderness.

Per Serving: Calories: 792, Total Fat: 76g, Total Carbs: 2g, Net Carbs: 2g, Fiber: 0g, Protein: 25g; Sodium: 783mg

Macros: Fat: 86%, Carbs: 1%, Protein: 13%

Caprese-Stuffed Chicken Breasts

EGG-FREE, GLUTEN-FREE, NUT-FREE

Serves 4
Prep Time: 20 minutes
Cook Time: 40 minutes

8 tablespoons extra-virgin olive oil, divided

2 boneless, skinless chicken breasts (about 6 ounces each)

4 ounces frozen spinach, thawed and drained well

1 cup shredded fresh mozzarella cheese

¼ cup chopped fresh basil

2 tablespoons chopped sun-dried tomatoes (preferably marinated in oil)

1 teaspoon salt, divided

1 teaspoon freshly ground black pepper, divided

½ teaspoon garlic powder

1 tablespoon balsamic vinegar

Found throughout Italian kitchens today, caprese salad originated in Capri, a small island nestled in the Bay of Naples in Italy. It is a wonderfully fresh summer dish, served best when tomatoes are at their peak of freshness. Here, I use sun-dried tomatoes for flavor as well as convenience. Rich in flavor, this is a fun spin on an Italian staple, which just so happens to look very similar to their country's flag!

1. Preheat the oven to 375°F.

2. Drizzle 1 tablespoon olive oil in a small deep baking dish and swirl to coat the bottom.

3. Make a deep incision about 3- to 4-inches long along the length of each chicken breast to create a pocket. Using your knife or fingers, carefully increase the size of the pocket without cutting through the chicken breast. (Each breast will look like a change purse with an opening at the top.)

4. In a medium bowl, combine the spinach, mozzarella, basil, sun-dried tomatoes, 2 tablespoons olive oil, ½ teaspoon salt, ½ teaspoon pepper, and the garlic powder and combine well with a fork.

(Recipe continues)

5. Stuff half of the filling mixture into the pocket of each chicken breast, stuffing down to fully fill the pocket. Press the opening together with your fingers. You can use a couple toothpicks to pin it closed if you wish.

6. In a medium skillet, heat 2 tablespoons olive oil over medium-high heat. Carefully sear the chicken breasts until browned, 3 to 4 minutes per side, being careful to not let too much filling escape. Transfer to the prepared baking dish, incision-side up. Scrape up any filling that fell out in the skillet and add it to baking dish. Cover the pan with foil and bake until the chicken is cooked through, 30 to 40 minutes, depending on the thickness of the breasts.

7. Remove from the oven and rest, covered, for 10 minutes. Meanwhile, in a small bowl, whisk together the remaining 3 tablespoons olive oil, balsamic vinegar, ½ teaspoon salt, and ½ teaspoon pepper.

8. To serve, cut each chicken breast in half, widthwise, and serve a half chicken breast drizzled with oil and vinegar.

Cooking Tip: Use the oil from the jarred sun-dried tomatoes in the filling for a delicious flavor boost, or try Garlic-Rosemary Infused Olive Oil (page 175) and omit the garlic powder.

Per Serving: Calories: 434, Total Fat: 35g, Total Carbs: 3g, Net Carbs: 2g, Fiber: 1g, Protein: 27g; Sodium: 742mg

Macros: Fat: 71%, Carbs: 3%, Protein: 26%

Lemon-Rosemary Spatchcock Chicken

DAIRY-FREE, EGG-FREE, GLUTEN-FREE, NUT-FREE

Serves 6 to 8
Prep Time: 20 minutes
Cook Time: 45 minutes

½ cup extra-virgin olive oil, divided

1 (3- to 4-pound) roasting chicken

8 garlic cloves, roughly chopped

2 to 4 tablespoons chopped fresh rosemary

2 teaspoons salt, divided

1 teaspoon freshly ground black pepper, divided

2 lemons, thinly sliced

While this might sound like a funny (or slightly off-color!) way to cook a chicken, it is actually a brilliant time-saver. Most roasted chickens take over an hour to cook fully and can bring anxiety, as no one wants to carve their bird only to find it still pink inside. Here, the bird is cut down the backbone so that it can be splayed flat for roasting, reducing cooking time while maintaining the flavorful, juicy meat that makes roasted chicken worth the fuss. You'll find detailed directions on how to spatchcock here, but you can also ask your butcher to do this for you.

1. Preheat the oven to 425°F.

2. Pour 2 tablespoons olive oil in the bottom of a 9-by-13-inch baking dish or rimmed baking sheet and swirl to coat the bottom.

3. To spatchcock the bird, place the whole chicken breast-side down on a large work surface. Using a very sharp knife, cut along the backbone, starting at the tail end and working your way up to the neck. Pull apart the two sides, opening up the chicken. Flip it over, breast-side up, pressing down with your hands to flatten the bird. Transfer to the prepared baking dish.

(Recipe continues)

4. Loosen the skin over the breasts and thighs by cutting a small incision and sticking one or two fingers inside to pull the skin away from the meat without removing it.

5. To prepare the filling, in a small bowl, combine ¼ cup olive oil, garlic, rosemary, 1 teaspoon salt, and ½ teaspoon pepper and whisk together.

6. Rub the garlic-herb oil evenly under the skin of each breast and each thigh. Add the lemon slices evenly to the same areas.

7. Whisk together the remaining 2 tablespoons olive oil, 1 teaspoon salt, and ½ teaspoon pepper and rub over the outside of the chicken.

8. Place in the oven, uncovered, and roast for 45 minutes, or until cooked through and golden brown. Allow to rest 5 minutes before carving to serve.

Substitution Tip: If you're in a hurry, you can create wonderfully tasty roasted chicken thighs using the same ingredients listed here. Just stuff the herb, garlic, oil, and lemon mixture under the skin of each thigh and roast for 25 to 30 minutes uncovered in the oven at 375°F.

Per Serving: Calories: 435, Total Fat: 34g, Total Carbs: 2g, Net Carbs: 2g, Fiber: 0g, Protein: 28g; Sodium: 879mg

Macros: Fat: 70%, Carbs: 2%, Protein: 28%

Lamb Kofte with Yogurt Sauce

EGG-FREE, GLUTEN-FREE

Serves 4
Prep Time: 30 minutes, plus 10 minutes to rest
Cook Time: 15 minutes

1 pound ground lamb
½ cup finely chopped fresh mint, plus 2 tablespoons
¼ cup almond or coconut flour
¼ cup finely chopped red onion
¼ cup toasted pine nuts
2 teaspoons ground cumin
1½ teaspoons salt, divided
1 teaspoon ground cinnamon
1 teaspoon ground ginger
½ teaspoon ground nutmeg
½ teaspoon freshly ground black pepper
1 cup plain whole-milk Greek yogurt
2 tablespoons extra-virgin olive oil
Zest and juice of 1 lime

Kofte are Middle Eastern–style lamb meatballs that are skewered, grilled, and served right on the skewer. They are traditionally made with bulgur wheat for binding, but they are delicious and even juicier without this addition. Here, I use a touch of almond or coconut flour to help them hold together. I find that broiling these in the oven, rather than grilling, also keeps them from losing their shape. The combination of warm savory spices with the light freshness of the mint is out of this world. For even easier cooking, you could simply make these into four patties and serve them with the yogurt sauce.

1. Heat the oven broiler to the low setting. You can also bake these at high heat (450 to 475°F) if you happen to have a very hot broiler. Submerge four wooden skewers in water and let soak at least 10 minutes to prevent them from burning.

2. In a large bowl, combine the lamb, ½ cup mint, almond flour, red onion, pine nuts, cumin, 1 teaspoon salt, cinnamon, ginger, nutmeg, and pepper and, using your hands, incorporate all the ingredients together well.

3. Form the mixture into 12 egg-shaped patties and let sit for 10 minutes.

(Recipe continues)

Lamb Kofte with Yogurt Sauce, continued

4. Remove the skewers from the water, thread 3 patties onto each skewer, and place on a broiling pan or wire rack on top of a baking sheet lined with aluminum foil. Broil on the top rack until golden and cooked through, 8 to 12 minutes, flipping once halfway through cooking.

5. While the meat cooks, in a small bowl, combine the yogurt, olive oil, remaining 2 tablespoons chopped mint, remaining ½ teaspoon salt, and lime zest and juice and whisk to combine well. Keep cool until ready to use.

6. Serve the skewers with yogurt sauce.

Substitution Tip: Lamb is a commonly used meat in Mediterranean cuisine, but not everyone is a fan. Feel free to substitute grass-fed ground beef if you prefer, although lamb is worth trying if you have not before. You're in for a treat!

Per Serving: Calories: 500, Total Fat: 42g, Total Carbs: 9g, Net Carbs: 7g, Fiber: 2g, Protein: 23g; Sodium: 969mg

Macros: Fat: 75%, Carbs: 6%, Protein: 19%

Meatballs in Creamy Almond Sauce

DAIRY-FREE, GLUTEN-FREE

Serves 4 to 6
Prp Time: 15 minutes
Cook Time: 35 minutes

8 ounces ground
  veal or pork
8 ounces ground beef
½ cup finely minced
  onion, divided
1 large egg, beaten
¼ cup almond flour
1½ teaspoons salt, divided
1 teaspoon garlic powder
½ teaspoon freshly ground
  black pepper
½ teaspoon ground nutmeg
2 teaspoons chopped fresh
  flat-leaf Italian parsley,
  plus ¼ cup, divided
½ cup extra-virgin olive
  oil, divided
¼ cup slivered almonds
1 cup dry white wine or
  chicken broth
¼ cup unsweetened
  almond butter

Albondigas, Spanish for meatballs, served in a signature sauce is a staple in every tapas restaurant in Madrid. Many use a tomato-based sauce, but one of the best I have ever used is a creamy almond-based sauce with a warm spice profile that was out of this world. So many Spanish sauce and soup recipes start with crumbled bread as their base or thickener. Here, I use almond flour along with almond butter instead. The white wine adds a wonderfully rich flavor, but feel free to use all chicken broth, if you prefer.

1. In a large bowl, combine the veal, beef, ¼ cup onion, and the egg and mix well with a fork. In a small bowl, whisk together the almond flour, 1 teaspoon salt, garlic powder, pepper, and nutmeg. Add to the meat mixture along with 2 teaspoons chopped parsley and incorporate well. Form the mixture into small meatballs, about 1 inch in diameter, and place on a plate. Let sit for 10 minutes at room temperature.

2. In a large skillet, heat ¼ cup oil over medium-high heat. Add the meatballs to the hot oil and brown on all sides, cooking in batches if necessary, 2 to 3 minutes per side. Remove from skillet and keep warm.

(Recipe continues)

Meatballs in Creamy Almond Sauce, continued

3. In the hot skillet, sauté the remaining ¼ cup minced onion in the remaining ¼ cup olive oil for 5 minutes. Reduce the heat to medium-low and add the slivered almonds. Sauté until the almonds are golden, another 3 to 5 minutes.

4. In a small bowl, whisk together the white wine, almond butter, and remaining ½ teaspoon salt. Add to the skillet and bring to a boil, stirring constantly. Reduce the heat to low, return the meatballs to skillet, and cover. Cook until the meatballs are cooked through, another 8 to 10 minutes.

5. Remove from the heat, stir in the remaining ¼ cup chopped parsley, and serve the meatballs warm and drizzled with almond sauce.

Leftovers Tip: You can double the amount of sauce that you make, freeze it, and use it to flavor other meats such as roasted chicken or pork. Slather boneless, skinless chicken thighs or pork chops in sauce, place them in a baking dish, cover, and bake at 375°F for 20 to 25 minutes, or until cooked through.

Per Serving: Calories: 449, Total Fat: 42g, Total Carbs: 3g, Net Carbs: 2g, Fiber: 1g, Protein: 16g; Sodium: 696mg

Macros: Fat: 83%, Carbs: 2%, Protein: 15%

Flank Steak with Orange-Herb Pistou

DAIRY-FREE, EGG-FREE, GLUTEN-FREE, NUT-FREE

Serves 4
Prep Time: 10 minutes
Cook Time: 20 minutes

1 pound flank steak

8 tablespoons extra-virgin
olive oil, divided

2 teaspoons salt, divided

1 teaspoon freshly ground
black pepper, divided

½ cup chopped fresh
flat-leaf Italian parsley

¼ cup chopped fresh
mint leaves

2 garlic cloves,
roughly chopped

Zest and juice of 1 orange or
2 clementines

1 teaspoon red pepper flakes
(optional)

1 tablespoon red
wine vinegar

This is a simple, yet impressive weeknight protein meal that comes together really quickly. The French version of pesto, pistou, can be used with any herb. I love the bright flavors of mint combined with orange here for a sauce very reminiscent of a South American chimichurri. I tend to double or even triple the quantities of any sauce or dressing I make to store extras for later in the week. This sauce is also light enough to use with a fish such as cod, halibut, and salmon.

1. Heat the grill to medium-high heat or, if using an oven, preheat to 400°F.

2. Rub the steak with 2 tablespoons olive oil and sprinkle with 1 teaspoon salt and ½ teaspoon pepper. Let sit at room temperature while you make the pistou.

3. In a food processor, combine the parsley, mint, garlic, orange zest and juice, remaining 1 teaspoon salt, red pepper flakes (if using), and remaining ½ teaspoon pepper. Pulse until finely chopped. With the processor running, stream in the red wine vinegar and remaining 6 tablespoons olive oil until well combined. This pistou will be more oil-based than traditional basil pesto.

(Recipe continues)

Flank Steak with Orange-Herb Pistou, continued

4. Cook the steak on the grill, 6 to 8 minutes per side. Remove from the grill and allow to rest for 10 minutes on a cutting board. If cooking in the oven, heat a large oven-safe skillet (cast iron works great) over high heat. Add the steak and sear, 1 to 2 minutes per side, until browned. Transfer the skillet to the oven and cook 10 to 12 minutes, or until the steak reaches your desired temperature.

5. To serve, slice the steak and drizzle with the pistou.

Leftovers Tip: Leftover steak is wonderful on top of a salad for an easy lunch. Drizzle with the pistou instead of dressing!

Per Serving: Calories: 441, Total Fat: 36g, Total Carbs: 3g, Net Carbs: 3g, Fiber: 0g, Protein: 25g; Sodium: 1237mg

Macros: Fat: 73%, Carbs: 3%, Protein: 24%

Moroccan Chicken and Vegetable Tagine

DAIRY-FREE, EGG-FREE, GLUTEN-FREE, NUT-FREE

Serves 6
Prep Time: 10 minutes
Cook Time: 1 hour

½ cup extra-virgin olive
   oil, divided
1½ pounds boneless skinless
   chicken thighs, cut into
   1-inch chunks
1½ teaspoons salt, divided
½ teaspoon freshly ground
   black pepper
1 small red onion, chopped
1 red bell pepper, cut into
   1-inch squares
2 medium tomatoes,
   chopped or 1½ cups diced
   canned tomatoes
1 cup water
2 medium zucchini, sliced
   into ¼-inch-thick
   half moons
1 cup pitted halved olives
   (Kalamata or Spanish
   green work nicely)
¼ cup chopped fresh
   cilantro or flat-leaf
   Italian parsley
Riced Cauliflower
   (page 177) or sautéed
   spinach, for serving

This is the perfect fall or winter one-pot dish to feed a crowd. As it cooks, the warm spicy smells fill up the house and just make me happy inside and out! This is wonderful served over a simple Riced Cauliflower (page 177), sautéed greens, or alongside a spinach salad dressed in Simple Vinaigrette (page 170).

1. In a Dutch oven or large rimmed skillet, heat ¼ cup olive oil over medium-high heat.

2. Season the chicken with 1 teaspoon salt and pepper and sauté until just browned on all sides, 6 to 8 minutes.

3. Add the onions and peppers and sauté until wilted, another 6 to 8 minutes.

4. Add the chopped tomatoes and water, bring to a boil, and reduce the heat to low. Cover and simmer over low heat until the meat is cooked through and very tender, 30 to 45 minutes.

5. Add the remaining ¼ cup olive oil, zucchini, olives, and cilantro, stirring to combine. Continue to cook over low heat, uncovered, until the zucchini is tender, about 10 minutes.

6. Serve warm over Riced Cauliflower (page 177) or atop a bed of sautéed spinach.

Per Serving: Calories: 358, Total Fat: 25g, Total Carbs: 8g, Net Carbs: 5g, Fiber: 3g, Protein: 25g; Sodium: 977mg

Macros: Fat: 63% Carbs: 8% Protein: 29%

One-Pan Harissa Chicken and Brussels Sprouts with Yogurt Sauce

EGG-FREE, GLUTEN-FREE, NUT-FREE

Serves 4
Prep Time: 10 minutes
Cook Time: 1 hour

8 tablespoons extra-virgin olive oil, divided

2 tablespoons Harissa Oil (page 173) or a store-bought harissa

1½ teaspoons salt, divided

½ teaspoon ground cumin

4 skin-on, bone-in chicken thighs (or a combination of thighs and drumsticks)

1 pound Brussels sprouts, ends trimmed and halved

½ cup plain whole-milk Greek yogurt

1 garlic clove, finely minced

Zest and juice of 1 lemon

½ cup chopped mint leaves, for serving

½ cup chopped cilantro leaves, for serving

The yogurt sauce mellows out the spiciness of the harissa in this easy weeknight meal. In my house, my husband and kids are on cleanup duty—I'm usually the mastermind behind the meal, after all, so it's only fair! I get extra love when this is on the menu. One pan means less mess! This meal is simple, yet pretty enough that it makes a nice presentation for company.

1. Preheat the oven to 425°F. Line a rimmed baking sheet with aluminum foil. (Alternatively, you can use a 9-by-13-inch glass baking dish and skip the foil.)

2. In a small bowl, whisk together 6 tablespoons olive oil, the harissa oil, 1 teaspoon salt, and cumin. Place the chicken in a large bowl and drizzle half of the harissa mixture over top. Toss to combine well. Place the chicken in a single layer on the prepared baking sheet and roast for 20 minutes.

3. While the chicken roasts, place the Brussels sprouts in a large bowl and drizzle with the remaining harissa mixture. Toss to combine well. After the chicken has roasted for 20 minutes, remove from the oven and add the Brussels sprouts to the baking sheet in a single layer around the chicken. Return to the oven and continue to roast until the chicken is cooked through and the Brussels sprouts are golden and crispy, another 20 to 25 minutes.

(Recipe continues)

4. In a small bowl, combine the yogurt, remaining 2 tablespoons olive oil, garlic, lemon zest and juice, and remaining ½ teaspoon salt and whisk to combine.

5. When the chicken and Brussels sprouts have finished cooking, remove from the oven and cool for 10 minutes. Drizzle with yogurt sauce and sprinkle with mint and cilantro. Toss to combine and serve warm.

Substitution Tip: If you don't have Harissa Oil (page 173) on hand, substitute 1 to 2 teaspoons red pepper flakes, 2 minced garlic cloves, and 2 table-spoons olive oil for the blend.

Per Serving: Calories: 607, Total Fat: 52g, Total Carbs: 13g, Net Carbs: 8g, Fiber: 5g, Protein: 25g; Sodium: 1002mg

Macros: Fat: 76%, Carbs: 8%, Protein: 16%

Stuffed Pork Loin with Sun-Dried Tomato and Goat Cheese

EGG-FREE, GLUTEN-FREE, NUT-FREE

Serves 6
Prep Time: 15 minutes
Cook Time: 30 to 40 minutes

1 to 1½ pounds pork
  tenderloin
1 cup crumbled goat cheese
4 ounces frozen spinach,
  thawed and well drained
2 tablespoons chopped
  sun-dried tomatoes
2 tablespoons extra-virgin
  olive oil (or seasoned
  oil marinade from
  sun-dried tomatoes),
  plus ¼ cup, divided
½ teaspoon salt
½ teaspoon freshly ground
  black pepper
Zucchini Noodles
  (page 176) or sautéed
  greens, for serving

I often cook with my clients in their homes to teach cooking techniques that can make their dietary needs and goals easier for them long-term. This recipe is a favorite! Not only because it is EASY and delicious, but because everyone loves to serve this for company and make believe they've spent hours in the kitchen. You'll need cooking twine or, in a pinch, unwaxed dental floss and toothpicks to make this come together beautifully.

1. Preheat the oven to 350°F. Cut cooking twine into eight (6-inch) pieces.

2. Cut the pork tenderloin in half lengthwise, leaving about an inch border, being careful to not cut all the way through to the other side. Open the tenderloin like a book to form a large rectangle. Place it between two pieces of parchment paper or plastic wrap and pound to about ¼-inch thickness with a meat mallet, rolling pin, or the back of a heavy spoon.

3. In a small bowl, combine the goat cheese, spinach, sun-dried tomatoes, 2 tablespoons olive oil, salt, and pepper and mix to incorporate well.

(Recipe continues)

4. Spread the filling over the surface of the pork, leaving a 1-inch border from one long edge and both short edges. To roll, start from the long edge with filling and roll towards the opposite edge. Tie cooking twine around the pork to secure it closed, evenly spacing each of the eight pieces of twine along the length of the roll.

5. In a Dutch oven or large oven-safe skillet, heat ¼ cup olive oil over medium-high heat. Add the pork and brown on all sides. Remove from the heat, cover, and bake until the pork is cooked through, 45 to 75 minutes, depending on the thickness of the pork. Remove from the oven and let rest for 10 minutes at room temperature.

6. To serve, remove the twine and discard. Slice the pork into medallions and serve over Zucchini Noodles (page 176) or sautéed greens, spooning the cooking oil and any bits of filling that fell out during cooking over top.

Substitution Tip: You can use flank steak in place of the pork, if you prefer. Cooking time will be slightly less, according to the final temperature you prefer.

Per Serving: Calories: 270, Total Fat: 21g, Total Carbs: 2g, Net Carbs: 1g, Fiber: 1g, Protein: 20g; Sodium: 323mg

Macros: Fat: 67% Carbs: 2% Protein: 31%

Chicken Piccata with Mushrooms

EGG-FREE, GLUTEN-FREE

Serves 4
Prep Time: 25 minutes
Cook Time: 25 minutes

1 pound thinly sliced
　chicken breasts
1½ teaspoons salt, divided
½ teaspoon freshly ground
　black pepper
¼ cup ground flaxseed
2 tablespoons almond flour
8 tablespoons extra-virgin
　olive oil, divided
4 tablespoons
　butter, divided
2 cups sliced mushrooms
½ cup dry white wine or
　chicken stock
¼ cup freshly squeezed
　lemon juice
¼ cup roughly
　chopped capers
Zucchini Noodles (page 176),
　for serving
¼ cup chopped fresh
　flat-leaf Italian parsley,
　for garnish

Piccata is an Italian style of cooking meat, usually chicken or veal, by dredging it in flour, panfrying, and then finishing in a tangy lemon sauce. To make this gluten-free and low in carbohydrates, this recipe uses the same traditional cooking method but substitutes ground flaxseed and almond flour for the white flour. The result is a rich and nutty flavor that works nicely with the acidity of the lemon and wine sauce. I've added mushrooms for variety, but you can keep them out if you don't have them on hand.

1. Season the chicken with 1 teaspoon salt and the pepper. On a plate, combine the ground flaxseed and almond flour and dredge each chicken breast in the mixture. Set aside.

2. In a large skillet, heat 4 tablespoons olive oil and 1 tablespoon butter over medium-high heat. Working in batches if necessary, brown the chicken, 3 to 4 minutes per side. Remove from the skillet and keep warm.

3. Add the remaining 4 tablespoons olive oil and 1 tablespoon butter to the skillet along with mushrooms and sauté over medium heat until just tender, 6 to 8 minutes.

(Recipe continues)

4. Add the white wine, lemon juice, capers, and remaining ½ teaspoon salt to the skillet and bring to a boil, whisking to incorporate any little browned bits that have stuck to the bottom of the skillet. Reduce the heat to low and whisk in the final 2 tablespoons butter.

5. Return the browned chicken to skillet, cover, and simmer over low heat until the chicken is cooked through and the sauce has thickened, 5 to 6 more minutes.

6. Serve chicken and mushrooms warm over Zucchini Noodles (page 176), spooning the mushroom sauce over top and garnishing with chopped parsley.

Prep Tip: This recipe calls for thinly sliced chicken breasts to allow for a quicker cooking time and crispy texture. Slice regular chicken breasts in half, lay them between two pieces of parchment, and pound them with a mallet to thin them out. However, most grocery stores also sell thinly sliced breasts, which are a bit more costly but can be a big time-saver.

Per Serving: Calories: 538, Total Fat: 44g, Total Carbs: 8g, Net Carbs: 5g, Fiber: 3g, Protein: 30g; Sodium: 1128mg

Macros: Fat: 74% Carbs: 4% Protein: 22%

Greek Chicken Souvlaki

DAIRY-FREE, EGG-FREE, GLUTEN-FREE, NUT-FREE

Serves 4
Prep Time: 10 minutes,
plus 1 hour to marinate
Cook Time: 15 minutes

½ cup extra-virgin olive oil,
   plus extra for serving
¼ cup dry white wine
   (optional; add extra lemon
   juice instead, if desired)
6 garlic cloves, finely minced
Zest and juice of 1 lemon
1 tablespoon dried oregano
1 teaspoon dried rosemary
½ teaspoons salt
½ teaspoon freshly ground
   black pepper
1 pound boneless, skinless
   chicken thighs, cut into
   1½-inch chunks
1 cup Tzatziki (page 168),
   for serving

> When I mentioned to one of my Greek clients that I was working on this cookbook, she asked me to come up with a great souvlaki recipe that wouldn't dry out. Using chicken thighs will make for a more tender dish, and the longer you allow the chicken to marinate before cooking, the tastier it will be.

1. In a large glass bowl or resealable plastic bag, combine the olive oil, white wine (if using), garlic, lemon zest and juice, oregano, rosemary, salt, and pepper and whisk or shake to combine well. Add the chicken to the marinade and toss to coat. Cover or seal and marinate in the refrigerator for at least 1 hour, or up to 24 hours.

2. In a bowl, submerge wooden skewers in water and soak for at least 30 minutes before using.

3. To cook, heat the grill to medium-high heat. Thread the marinated chicken on the soaked skewers, reserving the marinade.

4. Grill until cooked through, flipping occasionally so that the chicken cooks evenly, 5 to 8 minutes. Remove and keep warm.

5. Bring the reserved marinade to a boil in a small saucepan. Reduce the heat to low and simmer 3 to 5 minutes.

6. Serve chicken skewers drizzled with hot marinade, adding more olive oil if desired, and Tzatziki (page 168).

Per Serving: Calories: 677, Total Fat: 61g, Total Carbs: 8g, Net Carbs: 8g, Fiber: 0g, Protein: 26g; Sodium: 1615mg

Macros: Fat: 80% Carbs: 5% Protein: 15%

Pan-Fried Pork Chops with Peppers and Onions

DAIRY-FREE, EGG-FREE, GLUTEN-FREE, NUT-FREE

Serves 4
Prep Time: 5 minutes
Cook Time: 25 minutes

4 (4-ounce) pork chops, untrimmed

1 ½ teaspoons salt, divided

1 teaspoon freshly ground black pepper, divided

½ cup extra-virgin olive oil, divided

1 red or orange bell pepper, thinly sliced

1 green bell pepper, thinly sliced

1 small yellow onion, thinly sliced

2 teaspoons dried Italian herbs (such as oregano, parsley, or rosemary)

2 garlic cloves, minced

1 tablespoon balsamic vinegar

This is a very simple midweek meal that comes together in just under 30 minutes. Buy chops that are about ¾-inch thick for best results. Too thin and they will be tough and too thick will mean a longer cooking time, which will dry out the outer layer of the chops.

1.   Season the pork chops with 1 teaspoon salt and ½ teaspoon pepper.

2.   In a large skillet, heat ¼ cup olive oil over medium-high heat. Fry the pork chops in the oil until browned and almost cooked through but not fully cooked, 4 to 5 minutes per side, depending on the thickness of chops. Remove from the skillet and cover to keep warm.

3.   Pour the remaining ¼ cup olive oil in the skillet and sauté the sliced peppers, onions, and herbs over medium-high heat until tender, 6 to 8 minutes. Add the garlic, stirring to combine, and return the pork to skillet. Cover, reduce the heat to low, and cook for another 2 to 3 minutes, or until the pork is cooked through.

4.   Turn off the heat. Using a slotted spoon, transfer the pork, peppers, and onions to a serving platter. Add the vinegar to the oil in the skillet and whisk to combine well. Drizzle the vinaigrette over the pork and serve warm.

Per Serving: Calories: 508, Total Fat: 40g, Total Carbs: 8g, Net Carbs: 6g, Fiber: 2g, Protein: 31g; Sodium: 972mg

Macros: Fat: 71% Carbs: 5% Protein: 24%

Moroccan Stuffed Peppers

DAIRY-FREE, EGG-FREE, GLUTEN-FREE

Serves 4
Prep Time: 10 minutes
Cook Time: 30 minutes

¼ cup, plus 2 tablespoons
   extra-virgin olive
   oil, divided
2 large red bell peppers
1 pound ground beef
1 small onion, finely chopped
2 garlic cloves, minced
2 tablespoons chopped
   fresh sage or 2 teaspoons
   dried sage
1 teaspoon salt
1 teaspoon ground allspice
½ teaspoon freshly ground
   black pepper
½ cup chopped fresh
   flat-leaf Italian parsley
½ cup chopped baby
   arugula leaves
½ cup chopped walnuts
1 tablespoon freshly
   squeezed orange juice

These stuffed peppers have such a unique flavor and are a great way to impress guests. The combination of sage and warm spices feels very fall-like to me, and I love serving these as the weather starts to turn a bit cooler and I'm ready for savory comfort food.

1. Preheat the oven to 425°F.

2. Drizzle 1 tablespoon olive oil in a rimmed baking sheet and swirl to coat the bottom.

3. Remove the stems from the peppers and cut in half lengthwise, then remove the seeds and membranes. Place cut-side down on the prepared baking sheet and roast until just softened, 5 to 8 minutes. Remove from the oven and allow to cool.

4. Meanwhile, in a large skillet, heat 1 tablespoon olive oil over medium-high heat. Add the beef and onions and sauté until the meat is browned and cooked through, 8 to 10 minutes. Add the garlic, sage, salt, allspice, and pepper and sauté for 2 more minutes.

5. Remove from the heat and cool slightly. Stir in the parsley, arugula, walnuts, orange juice, and remaining ¼ cup olive oil and mix well.

6. Stuff the filling into each pepper half. Return to the oven and cook for 5 minutes. Serve warm.

Per Serving: Calories: 521, Total Fat: 44g, Total Carbs: 9g, Net Carbs: 6g, Fiber: 3g, Protein: 25g; Sodium: 665mg

Macros: Fat: 75%, Carbs: 6%, Protein: 19%

Sweet Treats

Chocolate Pudding

EGG-FREE, GLUTEN-FREE, NUT-FREE, VEGETARIAN

Serves 4

Prep Time: 10 minutes, plus 1 hour to chill

2 ripe avocados, halved and pitted

¼ cup unsweetened cocoa powder

¼ cup heavy whipping cream, plus more if needed

2 teaspoons vanilla extract

1 to 2 teaspoons liquid stevia or monk fruit extract (optional)

½ teaspoon ground cinnamon (optional)

¼ teaspoon salt

Whipped cream, for serving (optional)

This pudding uses avocado to create a heart-healthy rich, creamy texture. I like using a bit of heavy whipping cream to add to that creaminess, but you could make this a dairy-free pudding by substituting unsweetened almond milk or omitting it all together for a thicker texture. I make this for my kids (who love avocados but are a bit wary of them in dessert) and they have no idea it's not traditional pudding. Remember to only use as much sweetener as you need to taste, or you can leave it out completely if you desire!

1. Using a spoon, scoop out the ripe avocado into a blender or large bowl, if using an immersion blender. Mash well with a fork.

2. Add the cocoa powder, heavy whipping cream, vanilla, sweetener (if using), cinnamon (if using), and salt. Blend well until smooth and creamy, adding additional cream, 1 tablespoon at a time, if the mixture is too thick.

3. Cover and refrigerate for at least 1 hour before serving. Serve chilled with additional whipped cream, if desired.

Prep Tip: You want your avocados to be ripe, but overly ripe avocados take on a bitter taste and are not good in this recipe. Make sure they are slightly soft to the touch, but not too mushy or brown on the inside.

Per Serving: Calories: 230, Total Fat: 22g, Total Carbs: 10g, Net Carbs: 4g, Fiber: 6g, Protein: 3g; Sodium: 163mg

Macros: Fat: 83%, Carbs: 13%, Protein: 4%

Nut Butter Cup Fat Bomb

DAIRY-FREE, EGG-FREE, GLUTEN-FREE, VEGAN

Serves 8

Prep Time: 5 minutes, plus 12 hours to freeze

½ cup crunchy almond butter (no sugar added)

½ cup light fruity extra-virgin olive oil

¼ cup ground flaxseed

2 tablespoons unsweetened cocoa powder

1 teaspoon vanilla extract

1 teaspoon ground cinnamon (optional)

1 to 2 teaspoons sugar-free sweetener of choice (optional)

These are my Ketogenic Mediterranean version of a peanut butter cup, but full of healthy nutrition! Most sweet fat bomb recipes use coconut oil or butter, as these saturated fats are solid at room temperature and retain their shape. Unsaturated fats, such as olive and almond oil, are liquid at room temperature so you'll need to store these in the freezer and only take them out just before eating so they don't liquify.

1. In a mixing bowl, combine the almond butter, olive oil, flaxseed, cocoa powder, vanilla, cinnamon (if using), and sweetener (if using) and stir well with a spatula to combine. Mixture will be a thick liquid.

2. Pour into 8 mini muffin liners and freeze until solid, at least 12 hours. Store in the freezer to maintain their shape.

Substitution Tip: You could use avocado oil in place of the fruitier olive oil but be sure to not use a cooking olive oil as the flavor will be too harsh and not as "sweet." Feel free to use other tree nut butters in place of the almond butter. Natural peanut butter will work as well, but it can be more pro-inflammatory for some people, so I try to keep it at a minimum.

Per Serving (1 fat bomb): Calories: 240, Total Fat: 24g, Total Carbs: 5g, Net Carbs: 3g, Fiber: 2g, Protein: 3g; Sodium: 3mg

Macros: Fat: 88%, Carbs: 7%, Protein: 5%

Marzipan Fat Bomb

DAIRY-FREE, EGG-FREE, GLUTEN-FREE, VEGAN

Serves 8
Prep Time: 5 minutes

1½ cup finely ground
   almond flour
½ to 1 cup powdered
   sugar-free sweetener
   of choice
2 teaspoons almond extract
½ cup light fruity
   extra-virgin olive oil or
   avocado oil

Marzipan is a paste made from almonds that is used in baking and candies throughout Europe. When I lived in Spain, I remember visiting this adorable little bakery that had the cutest little marzipan bunnies at Easter. They looked almost too pretty to eat! What I love about it is the rich flavor that really doesn't even need to be sweet to enjoy. Start with only ½ cup of the sweetener and adjust, if needed. Make sure to look for powdered sugar-free sweetener for the right consistency.

1. Add the almond flour and sweetener to a food processor and run until the mixture is very finely ground.

2. Add the almond extract and pulse until combined. With the processor running, stream in olive oil until the mixture starts to form a large ball. Turn off the food processor.

3. Using your hands, form the marzipan into eight (1-inch) diameter balls, pressing to hold the mixture together. Store in an airtight container in the refrigerator for up to 2 weeks.

Substitution Tip: You can use vanilla extract in place of the almond extract if you don't have any on hand, but the almond flavor will be less pronounced.

Per Serving (1 fat bomb): Calories: 157, Total Fat: 17g, Total Carbs: 0g, Net Carbs: 0g, Fiber: 0g, Protein: 2g; Sodium: 0mg

Macros: Fat: 94%, Carbs: 2%, Protein: 4%

Strawberry Panna Cotta

EGG-FREE, GLUTEN-FREE, NUT-FREE

Serves 4
Prep Time: 10 minutes,
plus 6 hours to chill
Cook Time: 10 minutes

2 tablespoons warm water

2 teaspoons gelatin powder

2 cups heavy cream

1 cup sliced strawberries,
   plus more for garnish

1 to 2 tablespoons
   sugar-free sweetener of
   choice (optional)

1 ½ teaspoons pure
   vanilla extract

4 to 6 fresh mint leaves, for
   garnish (optional)

Panna cotta, common in Italy, is a cross between a gelatin and a pudding. Rather than using a custard base with eggs, the gelatin helps the dessert hold its shape. It is wonderfully delicious and a treat if you have never tried it before. Here, the pureed strawberries and rich cream give a great sweet flavor without needing any sweetener, so try it without any first. I love garnishing this with fresh mint or basil for a light summertime dessert.

1.   Pour the warm water into a small bowl. Sprinkle the gelatin over the water and stir well to dissolve. Allow the mixture to sit for 10 minutes.

2.   In a blender or a large bowl, if using an immersion blender, combine the cream, strawberries, sweetener (if using), and vanilla. Blend until the mixture is smooth and the strawberries are well puréed.

3.   Transfer the mixture to a saucepan and heat over medium-low heat until just below a simmer. Remove from the heat and cool for 5 minutes.

4.   Whisking constantly, add in the gelatin mixture until smooth. Divide the custard between ramekins or small glass bowls, cover and refrigerate until set, 4 to 6 hours.

5.   Serve chilled, garnishing with additional sliced strawberries or mint leaves (if using).

Per Serving: Calories: 431, Total Fat: 44g, Total Carbs: 7g, Net Carbs: 6g, Fiber: 1g, Protein: 4g; Sodium: 49mg

Macros: Fat: 90%, Carbs: 6%, Protein: 4%

Chocolate Chia Pudding

EGG-FREE, GLUTEN-FREE, NUT-FREE, VEGETARIAN

Serves 4

Prep Time: 10 minutes, plus 6 to 8 hours to chill

2 cups heavy cream

¼ cup unsweetened cocoa powder

1 teaspoon almond extract or vanilla extract

½ or 1 teaspoon ground cinnamon

¼ teaspoon salt

½ cup chia seeds

High in omega-3 fatty acids and fiber, chia seeds are a great addition to any ketogenic diet. When added to liquids, such as in smoothies or in this pudding, they create a gummy texture that acts much like a gelatin would in a pudding. It is important to warm the cream prior to adding the cocoa powder, or it will not dissolve into the liquid and you will be left with chalky clumps.

1. In a saucepan, heat the heavy cream over medium-low heat to just below a simmer. Remove from the heat and allow to cool slightly.

2. In a blender or large bowl, if using an immersion blender, combine the warmed heavy cream, cocoa powder, almond extract, cinnamon, and salt and blend until the cocoa is well incorporated.

3. Stir in the chia seeds and let sit for 15 minutes.

4. Divide the mixture evenly between ramekins or small glass bowls and refrigerate at least 6 hours, or until set. Serve chilled.

Substitution Tip: You can change up the flavors of this easy pudding in a snap. Try a berry version by replacing ¼ cocoa powder with pureed berries and omitting the cinnamon, or try a nutty version by adding in ¼ cup almond or hazelnut butter. The possibilities are endless!

Per Serving: Calories: 561, Total Fat: 53g, Total Carbs: 19g, Net Carbs: 7g, Fiber: 12g, Protein: 8g; Sodium: 187mg

Macros: Fat: 83%, Carbs: 12%, Protein: 5%

Orange-Olive Oil Cupcakes

DAIRY-FREE, GLUTEN-FREE, VEGETARIAN

Makes 6 cupcakes
Prep Time: 15 minutes
Cook Time: 20 minutes

1 large egg
2 tablespoons powdered
sugar-free sweetener (such
as stevia or monk fruit
extract)
½ cup extra-virgin olive oil
1 teaspoon almond extract
Zest of 1 orange
1 cup almond flour
¾ teaspoon baking powder
⅛ teaspoon salt
1 tablespoon freshly
squeezed orange juice

Full of heart-healthy unsaturated fats from the olive oil and almond flour, these cupcakes are about as healthy as dessert can get and the strong orange flavor is out of this world! These are tasty and satisfying on their own, or you can serve them with a dollop of whipped cream or berry syrup for a beautiful presentation. Again, make sure to use a fruity olive oil in desserts for the best flavor. These will keep in the freezer for up to 2 months, so no need to eat the whole batch at once!

1. Preheat the oven to 350°F. Place muffin liners into 6 cups of a muffin tin.

2. In a large bowl, whisk together the egg and powdered sweetener. Add the olive oil, almond extract, and orange zest and whisk to combine well.

3. In a small bowl, whisk together the almond flour, baking powder, and salt. Add to wet ingredients along with the orange juice and stir until just combined.

4. Divide the batter evenly into 6 muffin cups and bake until a toothpick inserted in the center of the cupcake comes out clean, 15 to 18 minutes.

5. Remove from the oven and cool for 5 minutes in the tin before transferring to a wire rack to cool completely.

Substitution Tip: These would also be delicious with grapefruit zest and juice in place of the orange. You can increase the amount of sweetener to your taste.

Per Serving: Calories: 211, Total Fat: 22g, Total Carbs: 2g, Net Carbs: 2g, Fiber: 0g, Protein: 3g; Sodium: 105mg

Macros: Fat: 91%, Carbs: 4%, Protein: 5%

Olive Oil Ice Cream

GLUTEN-FREE, NUT-FREE, VEGETARIAN

Serves 8
Prep Time: 5 minutes, plus 12 to 24 hours inactive time
Cook Time: 25 minutes, plus 6 hours to chill

4 large egg yolks
⅓ cup powdered sugar-free sweetener (such as stevia or monk fruit extract)
2 cups half-and-half or 1 cup heavy whipping cream and 1 cup whole milk
1 teaspoon vanilla extract
⅛ teaspoon salt
¼ cup light fruity extra-virgin olive oil

> It may sound like a crazy combination, but this ice cream is AMAZING—trust me!

1. Freeze the bowl of an ice cream maker for at least 12 hours or overnight.

2. In a large bowl, whisk together the egg yolks and sugar-free sweetener.

3. In a small saucepan, heat the half-and-half over medium heat until just below a boil. Remove from the heat and allow to cool slightly.

4. Slowly pour the warm half-and-half into the egg mixture, whisking constantly to avoid cooking the eggs. Return the eggs and cream to the saucepan over low heat.

5. Whisking constantly, cook over low heat until thickened, 15 to 20 minutes. Remove from the heat and stir in the vanilla extract and salt. Whisk in the olive oil and transfer to a glass bowl. Allow to cool, cover, and refrigerate for at least 6 hours.

6. Freeze custard in an ice cream maker according to manufacturer's directions.

Prep Tip: To make this without an ice cream maker, prepare the custard according to directions. Refrigerate at least 12 hours. Using an electric mixer, whip the custard until doubled in volume. Freeze for at least 6 hours before serving.

Per Serving: Calories: 292, Total Fat: 31g, Total Carbs: 2g, Net Carbs: 2g, Fiber: 0g, Protein: 3g; Sodium: 63mg

Macros: Fat: 94%, Carbs: 2%, Protein: 4%

Pumpkin-Ricotta Cheesecake

GLUTEN-FREE, VEGETARIAN

Serves 10 to 12

Prep Time: 25 minutes, plus 6 hours to set

Cook Time: 45 minutes

1 cup almond flour

½ cup butter, melted

1 (14.5-ounce) can pumpkin purée

8 ounces cream cheese, at room temperature

½ cup whole-milk ricotta cheese

½ to ¾ cup sugar-free sweetener

4 large eggs

2 teaspoons vanilla extract

2 teaspoons pumpkin pie spice

Whipped cream, for garnish (optional)

> In Spain, they use *calabaza* (pumpkin) to make rich soups and sauces. In Italian cuisine, ricotta is often used in desserts. I like to think of this cheesecake as the best of both worlds, and this would be a great Mediterranean addition to an American Thanksgiving.

1. Preheat the oven to 350°F. Line the bottom of a 9-inch springform pan with parchment paper.

2. In a small bowl, combine the almond flour and melted butter with a fork until well combined. Using your fingers, press the mixture into the bottom of the prepared pan.

3. In a large bowl, beat together the pumpkin purée, cream cheese, ricotta, and sweetener using an electric mixer on medium.

4. Add the eggs, one at a time, beating after each addition. Stir in the vanilla and pumpkin pie spice until just combined.

5. Pour the mixture over the crust and bake until set, 40 to 45 minutes.

6. Allow to cool to room temperature. Refrigerate for at least 6 hours before serving.

7. Serve chilled, garnishing with whipped cream, if desired.

Per Serving: Calories: 242, Total Fat: 22g, Total Carbs: 5g, Net Carbs: 4g, Fiber: 1g, Protein: 7g; Sodium: 178mg

Macros: Fat: 81%, Carbs: 8%, Protein: 11%

CHAPTER TEN

Staples, Sauces, and Dressings

Arugula and Walnut Pesto

EGG-FREE, GLUTEN-FREE, VEGETARIAN

Serves 8 to 10
Prep Time: 5 minutes

6 cups packed arugula
1 cup chopped walnuts
½ cup shredded
   Parmesan cheese
2 garlic cloves, peeled
½ teaspoon salt
1 cup extra-virgin olive oil

This is a wonderful and refreshing alternative to traditional basil and pine nut pesto and is a great way to use up excess arugula that is getting ready to turn. The micronutrient-rich superfood arugula combined with the high amount of healthy fats in the walnuts is a powerhouse combination that is wonderful over simple Zucchini Noodles (page 176), as a topping for scrambled eggs, or as a sandwich spread. The cheese helps to create a creamy texture, but feel free to omit it for a dairy-free version. You could also substitute in nutritional yeast flakes if you have those on hand.

1. In a food processor, combine the arugula, walnuts, cheese, and garlic and process until very finely chopped. Add the salt. With the processor running, stream in the olive oil until well blended.

2. If the mixture seems too thick, add warm water, 1 tablespoon at a time, until smooth and creamy. Store in a sealed container in the refrigerator.

Per Serving (2 tablespoons): Calories: 296, Total Fat: 31g, Total Carbs: 3g, Net Carbs: 2g, Fiber: 1g, Protein: 4g; Sodium: 206mg

Macros: Fat: 91%, Carbs: 4%, Protein: 5%

Creamy Grapefruit-Tarragon Dressing

DAIRY-FREE, GLUTEN-FREE, NUT-FREE, VEGETARIAN

Serves 4 to 6
Prep Time: 5 minutes

½ cup avocado oil
  mayonnaise or Homemade
  Aioli (page 166–167)
2 tablespoons Dijon mustard
1 teaspoon dried tarragon
  or 1 tablespoon chopped
  fresh tarragon
Zest and juice of
  ½ grapefruit (about
  2 tablespoons juice)
½ teaspoon salt
¼ teaspoon freshly ground
  black pepper
1 to 2 tablespoons water
  (optional)

This refreshing, creamy dressing is wonderful on summer salads and is full of healthy omega-3 fatty acids. I like using avocado mayonnaise for its healthy fat profile, as most store-bought traditional mayonnaises use pro-inflammatory canola oil. You can use a Homemade Aioli (page 166–167) as well for high levels of omega-3s. Fresh tarragon can be hard to find out of season, so I always keep dried on hand.

In a large mason jar or glass measuring cup, combine the mayonnaise, Dijon, tarragon, grapefruit zest and juice, salt, and pepper and whisk well with a fork until smooth and creamy. If a thinner dressing is preferred, thin out with water.

Substitution Tip: I love the flavor combination of grapefruit and tarragon, but you can substitute another herb, such as rosemary or basil, for the tarragon if you prefer. Add poppy or chia seeds for a little crunch.

Per Serving (2 tablespoons): Calories: 86, Total Fat: 7g, Total Carbs: 6g, Net Carbs: 6g, Fiber: 0g, Protein: 1g; Sodium: 390mg

Macros: Fat: 69%, Carbs: 29%, Protein: 2%

Bagna Cauda

EGG-FREE, GLUTEN-FREE, NUT-FREE

Serves 8 to 10
Prep Time: 5 minutes
Cook Time: 20 minutes

½ cup extra-virgin olive oil
4 tablespoons
   (½ stick) butter
8 anchovy fillets, very
   finely chopped
4 large garlic cloves,
   finely minced
½ teaspoon salt
½ teaspoon freshly ground
   black pepper

Translated from Italian, *bagna cauda* literally means "hot bath" and is a sauce traditionally served on Christmas Eve. I love the visual of this intensely flavorful sauce being a "hot bath" for whatever I'm serving it with. It makes a wonderful accompaniment for steamed fresh artichokes. I like to keep a batch of this in my fridge to drizzle over simple weeknight veggies or to use as a dipping sauce for crab or lobster. It is both decadent and delicious!

1. In a small saucepan, heat the olive oil and butter over medium-low heat until the butter is melted.

2. Add the anchovies and garlic and stir to combine. Add the salt and pepper and reduce the heat to low. Cook, stirring occasionally, until the anchovies are very soft and the mixture is very fragrant, about 20 minutes.

3. Serve warm, drizzled over steamed vegetables, as a dipping sauce for raw veggies or cooked artichokes, or use as a salad dressing. Store leftovers in an airtight container in the refrigerator for up to 2 weeks.

Per Serving (2 tablespoons): Calories: 181, Total Fat: 20g, Total Carbs: 1g, Net Carbs: 1g, Fiber: 0g, Protein: 1g; Sodium: 333mg

Macros: Fat: 96%, Carbs: 1%, Protein: 3%

Lemon-Tahini Dressing

DAIRY-FREE, EGG-FREE, GLUTEN-FREE, NUT-FREE, VEGAN

Serves 8 to 10
Prep Time: 5 minutes

½ cup tahini
¼ cup freshly squeezed
   lemon juice (about 2 to
   3 lemons)
¼ cup extra-virgin olive oil
1 garlic clove, finely
   minced or ½ teaspoon
   garlic powder
2 teaspoons salt

Tahini is a paste made from ground sesame seeds. Commonly used in Mediterranean cuisines, it is what gives hummus its creamy texture. It can be found jarred or canned in the ethnic foods or nut butter aisle of most grocery stores. Once opened, it can be stored in the refrigerator for several months. Make sure to stir the tahini well before using, as it separates easily. This dressing is great with grilled or roasted chicken or on tuna over simple greens.

In a glass mason jar with a lid, combine the tahini, lemon juice, olive oil, garlic, and salt. Cover and shake well until combined and creamy. Store in the refrigerator for up to 2 weeks.

Per Serving (2 tablespoons): Calories: 121, Total Fat: 12g, Total Carbs: 3g, Net Carbs: 2g, Fiber: 1g, Protein: 2g; Sodium: 479mg

Macros: Fat: 84%, Carbs: 10%, Protein: 6%

Homemade Aioli, Two Ways: Zesty Orange and Roasted Garlic

DAIRY-FREE, GLUTEN-FREE, NUT-FREE, VEGETARIAN

Aioli is a great mayonnaise alternative. The Spanish word for garlic is *ajo*, and for oil, *olio*. Aioli is a beautiful marriage between garlic and oil with the addition of eggs to make it creamy. Be sure to use a light, fruity olive oil rather than one with a stronger flavor for the best results.

Zesty Orange Aioli

Serves 8 to 10
Prep Time: 5 minutes,
plus 1 hour to rest

2 large egg yolks
2 garlic cloves, finely minced
Zest and juice of 1 orange
1 ½ teaspoons salt
1 teaspoon red pepper flakes
1 cup extra-virgin olive oil

1. In a blender or large bowl, if using an immersion blender, combine the egg yolks, garlic, orange zest and juice, salt, and red pepper flakes and pulse until well combined and pasty.

2. With the blender running, stream in the olive oil until just combined. Let sit at room temperature at least 1 hour before serving. Store in the refrigerator.

Per Serving (2 tablespoons): Calories: 203, Total Fat: 23g, Total Carbs: 0g, Net Carbs: 0g, Fiber: 0g, Protein: 1g; Sodium: 351mg

Macros: Fat: 98%, Carbs: 1%, Protein: 1%

Roasted Garlic Aioli

Serves 8 to 10
Prep Time: 5 minutes,
plus 1 hour to rest
Cook Time: 45 minutes

1 small head garlic, unpeeled
1 tablespoon extra-virgin olive oil,
   plus 1 cup, divided
2 large egg yolks
4 teaspoons freshly squeezed
   lemon juice
1 ½ teaspoons salt

1. Preheat the oven to 375°F.

2. Cut the top ½ inch off the unpeeled head of garlic so that the cloves are exposed. Brush with 1 tablespoon olive oil and wrap in foil. Place the foil bundle on a baking sheet and bake until very soft, 40 to 45 minutes.

3. Allow the garlic to cool before handling. Remove the roasted garlic by squeezing the cloves from their skins into a blender or, if using an immersion blender, a medium bowl.

4. Add the egg yolks, lemon juice, and salt to the garlic and pulse until combined and a paste has formed. With the blender running, stream in the remaining 1 cup olive oil until just combined. Let sit at room temperature at least 1 hour before serving. Store in the refrigerator.

Per Serving (2 tablespoons): Calories: 218, Total Fat: 24g, Total Carbs: 1g, Net Carbs: 1g, Fiber: 0g, Protein: 1g; Sodium: 351mg

Macros: Fat: 97% Carbs: 2% Protein: 1%

Tzatziki

EGG-FREE, GLUTEN-FREE, NUT-FREE, VEGETARIAN

Serves 4 to 6
Prep Time: 5 minutes, plus 15 minutes to drain

½ English cucumber, finely chopped
1 teaspoon salt, divided
1 cup plain whole-milk Greek yogurt
8 tablespoons olive oil (preferably Greek), divided
1 to 2 tablespoons chopped fresh dill or 1 to 2 teaspoons dried dill
1 garlic clove, finely minced
1 teaspoon red wine vinegar
½ teaspoon freshly ground black pepper

You'll find this cool and creamy condiment served with just about every dish in Greek cuisine. There's not much it doesn't pair nicely with! This recipe uses more olive oil than the traditional version to offset the higher protein-to-fat ratio from the yogurt.

1. In a food processor or blender, pulse the cucumber until puréed. Place the cucumber on several layers of paper towels lining the bottom of a colander and sprinkle with ½ teaspoon salt. Allow to drain for 10 to 15 minutes. Using your hands, squeeze out any remaining liquid and pat dry.

2. In a medium bowl, whisk together the cucumber, yogurt, 6 tablespoons olive oil, dill, garlic, vinegar, remaining ½ teaspoon salt, and pepper until very smooth.

3. Drizzle the remaining 2 tablespoons olive oil over the top of dip prior to serving. Store in the refrigerator.

Prep Tip: You can skip the step of draining the puréed cucumber, but the resulting dip will be watery. Sometimes this is a nice consistency to use as a dressing, but for a thicker dip to use with veggies or along with skewered meats and fish, you will want to be sure not to skip the draining!

Per Serving (¼ cup): Calories: 286, Total Fat: 29g, Total Carbs: 5g, Net Carbs: 5g, Fiber: 0g, Protein: 3g; Sodium: 615mg

Macros: Fat: 90%, Carbs: 6%, Protein: 4%

Versatile Sandwich Round

DAIRY-FREE, GLUTEN-FREE, VEGETARIAN

Serves 1
Prep Time: 5 minutes
Cook Time: 90 seconds

3 tablespoons almond flour
1 tablespoon extra-virgin olive oil
1 large egg
½ teaspoon dried rosemary, oregano, basil, thyme, or garlic powder (optional)
¼ teaspoon baking powder
⅛ teaspoon salt

This keto-friendly bread is a cross between an English muffin and a sandwich round. You can skip the slicing and use it as a dinner roll or opt to very thinly slice it and toast it in the oven to create more of a cracker texture for serving with a charcuterie platter. The possibilities are endless! These are so quick to make that you can whip one up just before serving, but if you choose to make a larger batch, store them in the fridge until you are ready to use them.

1. In a microwave-safe ramekin, combine the almond flour, olive oil, egg, rosemary (if using), baking powder, and salt. Mix well with a fork.

2. Microwave for 90 seconds on high.

3. Slide a knife around the edges of ramekin and flip to remove the bread.

4. Slice in half with a serrated knife if you want to use it to make a sandwich.

Substitution Tip: You can make a sweet version of this bread using coconut or almond flour and butter in place of the oil. Flavor with cinnamon or nutmeg and a touch of vanilla extract.

Per Serving: Calories: 232, Total Fat: 22g, Total Carbs: 1g, Net Carbs: 0g, Fiber: 0g, Protein: 8g; Sodium: 450mg

Macros: Fat: 84%, Carbs: 2%, Protein: 14%

Simple Vinaigrette

DAIRY-FREE, EGG-FREE, GLUTEN-FREE, NUT-FREE, VEGAN

Makes 1 cup
Prep Time: 5 minutes

½ cup extra-virgin olive oil
¼ cup red wine vinegar
  or freshly squeezed
  lemon juice
1 tablespoon Dijon mustard
1 small garlic clove, finely
  minced (optional)
1 teaspoon dried herbs
  (oregano, rosemary,
  parsley, or thyme)
½ teaspoon salt
½ teaspoon freshly ground
  black pepper

A vinaigrette is really just a combination of an oil and an acid. Here, I use extra-virgin olive oil and red wine vinegar, although you can use lemon juice for a bolder taste. Most store-bought dressings, even those that don't contain sugar, are made with canola and/or soybean oil as their base which is pro-inflammatory and not nearly as tasty as olive oil. Combine the health benefits of making your own with the money-saving bonus and you'll never buy bottled dressing again!

In a glass Mason jar with a lid, combine the olive oil, vinegar, Dijon, garlic (if using), herbs, salt, and pepper and shake until well combined. Store in the refrigerator and bring to room temperature before serving. Be sure to shake the dressing well before using as the oil and vinegar will naturally separate.

Per Serving (2 tablespoons): Calories: 124, Total Fat: 14g, Total Carbs: 1g, Net Carbs: 1g, Fiber: 0g, Protein: 0g; Sodium: 170mg

Macros: Fat: 97%, Carbs: 2%, Protein: 1%

Homemade Marinara

EGG-FREE, GLUTEN-FREE, NUT-FREE, VEGETARIAN

Makes 8 cups
Prep Time: 15 minutes
Cook Time: 40 minutes to
1 hour 10 minutes

1 small onion, diced
1 small red bell pepper,
    stemmed, seeded
    and chopped
2 tablespoons plus
    ¼ cup extra-virgin olive
    oil, divided
2 tablespoons butter
4 to 6 garlic cloves, minced
2 teaspoon salt, divided
½ teaspoon freshly ground
    black pepper
2 (32-ounce) cans crushed
    tomatoes (with basil, if
    possible), with their juices
½ cup thinly sliced basil
    leaves, divided
2 tablespoons chopped
    fresh rosemary
1 to 2 teaspoons crushed red
    pepper flakes (optional)

This is a great base for a number of the recipes in this book and, served over a bed of Zucchini Noodles (page 176), makes for a super-easy weeknight meal. Most store-bought marinara sauces not only lack the flavor of homemade but are loaded with sugar, making them not keto-friendly. This version is flavor-forward and doesn't hide any of the fresh taste with added sugar.

1. In a food processor, combine the onion and bell pepper and blend until very finely minced.

2. In a large skillet, heat 2 tablespoons olive oil and the butter over medium heat. Add the minced onion, and red pepper and sauté until just starting to get tender, about 5 minutes.

3. Add the garlic, salt, and pepper and sauté until fragrant, another 1 to 2 minutes.

4. Reduce the heat to low and add the tomatoes and their juices, remaining ¼ cup olive oil, ¼ cup basil, rosemary, and red pepper flakes (if using). Stir to combine, then bring to a simmer and cover. Cook over low heat for 30 to 60 minutes to allow the flavors to blend.

5. Add remaining ¼ cup chopped fresh basil after removing from heat, stirring to combine.

Per Serving (1 cup): Calories: 265, Total Fat: 20g, Total Carbs: 19g, Net Carbs: 14g, Fiber: 5g, Protein: 4g; Sodium: 803mg

Macros: Fat: 70%, Carbs: 24%, Protein: 6%

Marinated Artichokes

DAIRY-FREE, EGG-FREE, GLUTEN-FREE, NUT-FREE, VEGAN

Makes 2 cups
Prep Time: 10 minutes,
plus 24 hours to marinate

2 (13.75-ounce) cans
   artichoke hearts, drained
   and quartered
¾ cup extra-virgin olive oil
4 small garlic cloves,
   crushed with the back
   of a knife
1 tablespoon fresh
   rosemary leaves
2 teaspoons chopped fresh
   oregano or 1 teaspoon
   dried oregano
1 teaspoon red pepper flakes
   (optional)
1 teaspoon salt

You'll find an assortment of veggies like carrots, pearl onions, artichokes, mushrooms, and beans marinated in a rich combination of olive oil, garlic, and fresh herbs on antipasto platters served throughout the Mediterranean. You can buy pre-marinated artichokes in many specialty markets here in the United States but they can be very pricey. Once you realize how easy it is to marinate your own, you won't think twice about buying premade again!

1. In a medium bowl, combine the artichoke hearts, olive oil, garlic, rosemary, oregano, red pepper flakes (if using), and salt. Toss to combine well.

2. Store in an airtight glass container in the refrigerator and marinate for at least 24 hours before using. Store in the refrigerator for up to 2 weeks.

Substitution Tip: You can use the same process and marinade for a variety of veggies. Try this with button mushrooms, pearl onions, or a combination of veggies for diversity.

Per Serving (¼ cup): Calories: 275, Total Fat: 27g, Total Carbs: 11g, Net Carbs: 7g, Fiber: 4g, Protein: 4g; Sodium: 652mg

Macros: Fat: 88%, Carbs: 7%, Protein: 5%

Harissa Oil

DAIRY-FREE, EGG-FREE, GLUTEN-FREE, NUT-FREE, VEGAN

Makes 1 cup
Prep Time: 15 minutes,
plus 30 minutes to steep
Cook Time: 5 minutes

4 to 6 medium-hot dried
   chiles (ancho or guajillo
   work well)
2 to 4 hot dried chiles de
   árbol (optional; these are
   very hot)
2 tablespoons
   coriander seeds
1 tablespoon cumin seeds
1 teaspoon caraway seeds
4 large garlic
   cloves, chopped
2 tablespoons tomato paste
2 teaspoons smoked paprika
1 teaspoon salt
1 cup extra-virgin olive
   oil, divided

Harissa is a wonderful North African condiment that can add intense flavor to many dishes. It typically has a pasty consistency, but this version is more like a fiery oil that can be used as a marinade or drizzled over cooked fish, meats, eggs, and vegetables. You can balance the heat to your preference by adjusting the amount and type of dried chile peppers used: *Chile de árbol* lends a wonderful heat but can be too spicy for some, while dried chipotle peppers would make a nice smoky version. This will keep well in the refrigerator up to 3 weeks.

1. Remove the stems and tops from the dried chiles and discard any loose seeds. Place the chiles in a bowl and cover with boiling water. Allow to steep 30 minutes or until softened. Remove from the water, drain off any excess liquid, and roughly chop, discarding any seeds and membranes. Set aside.

2. In a dry skillet, toast the coriander, cumin, and caraway seeds over medium-high heat until very fragrant. Transfer to the bowl of a food processer or blender.

3. Add the chopped chiles, garlic, tomato paste, paprika, and salt and pulse until a thick paste forms.

(Recipe continues)

Harissa Oil, continued

4. With the food processor or blender running, stream in ¾ cup olive oil until well combined. Transfer to large glass jar and stir in the remaining ¼ cup olive oil. Store in an airtight container in the refrigerator for up to 3 weeks.

Substitution Tip: If you're short on time or having trouble finding whole dried chiles, ¼ cup red pepper flakes can be substituted in a pinch.

Per Serving (2 tablespoons): Calories: 266, Total Fat: 26g, Total Carbs: 6g, Net Carbs: 5g, Fiber: 1g, Protein: 2g; Sodium: 299mg

Macros: Fat: 88%, Carbs: 9%, Protein: 3%

Garlic-Rosemary Infused Olive Oil

DAIRY-FREE, EGG-FREE, GLUTEN-FREE, NUT-FREE, VEGAN

Makes 1 cup
Prep Time: 5 minutes
Cook Time: 45 minutes

1 cup extra-virgin olive oil
4 large garlic
   cloves, smashed
4 (4- to 5-inch) sprigs
   rosemary

An easy way to add great healthy fats to your diet is to drizzle those micronutrient-dense veggies with quality olive oil. Flavored oils can be found in gourmet markets, but often you are paying a high price for low-quality oil. I prefer to make my own with my favorite high-quality oil to keep on hand for all occasions.

1.   In a medium skillet, heat the olive oil, garlic, and rosemary sprigs over low heat. Cook until fragrant and garlic is very tender, 30 to 45 minutes, stirring occasionally. Don't let the oil get too hot or the garlic will burn and become bitter.

2.   Remove from the heat and allow to cool slightly. Remove the garlic and rosemary with a slotted spoon and pour the oil into a glass container. Allow to cool completely before covering. Store covered at room temperature for up to 3 months.

Substitution Tip: Once you master the technique of making infused oils, you can vary the herbs and spices to your palate. You can use thyme or any other hearty herb in place of the rosemary and add red pepper flakes for a spicier oil.

Per Serving (2 tablespoons): Calories: 241, Total Fat: 27g, Total Carbs: 1g, Net Carbs: 1g, Fiber: 0g, Protein: 0g; Sodium: 1mg

Macros: Fat: 99%, Carbs: 1%, Protein: 0%

Zucchini Noodles

DAIRY-FREE, EGG-FREE, GLUTEN-FREE, NUT-FREE, VEGAN

Serves 4
Prep Time: 5 minutes

2 medium to large zucchini

This is less of a recipe and more of a how-to! Zucchini "noodles," or zoodles, are a staple in low-carb and pasta-free cooking. I love the versatility of these for serving under any delicious sauce or even a hearty stew. For the perfect al dente zucchini noodle, the trick is to not cook them. Cooking or sautéing the zoodles prior to serving will only make them soggy and limp, and they'll lack the ability to soak up any yummy sauce.

1. Cut off and discard the ends of each zucchini and, using a spiralizer set to the smallest setting, spiralize the zucchini to create zoodles.

2. To serve, simply place a ½ cup or so of spiralized zucchini into the bottom of each bowl and spoon a hot sauce over top to "cook" the zoodles to al dente consistency. Use with any of your favorite sauces, or just toss with warmed pesto for a simple and quick meal.

Leftovers Tip: Spiralized zoodles will keep in the refrigerator for 1 to 2 days, but I find that they lose their crunch if kept much longer than that and they do not freeze well. These are best made just before serving.

Per Serving: Calories: 48, Total Fat: 1g, Total Carbs: 7g, Net Carbs: 4g, Fiber: 3g, Protein: 6g; Sodium: 7mg

Macros: Fat: 16%, Carbs: 53%, Protein: 31%

Riced Cauliflower

DAIRY-FREE, EGG-FREE, GLUTEN-FREE, NUT-FREE, VEGAN

Serves 6 to 8
Prep Time: 5 minutes
Cook Time: 10 minutes

1 small head cauliflower,
   broken into florets
¼ cup extra-virgin olive oil
2 garlic cloves, finely minced
1 ½ teaspoons salt
½ teaspoon freshly ground
   black pepper

When chopped very finely with a food processor or grated with a box grater, cauliflower has an amazing ability to mimic the consistency of rice or couscous. So versatile and loved is this substitution that many companies are now making preprepared riced cauliflower that you can buy either fresh or frozen. Like any vegetable, cauliflower has a high water content not inherent to rice or dried pasta, and many of these convenience options result in a mushy consistency that can immediately turn off a potential convert. Making your own is so easy, inexpensive, and flavor-preserving. This easy preparation makes a simple riced cauliflower, but feel free to add spices and herbs to create different flavor profiles.

1. Place the florets in a food processor and pulse several times, until the cauliflower is the consistency of rice or couscous.

2. In a large skillet, heat the olive oil over medium-high heat. Add the cauliflower, garlic, salt, and pepper and sauté for 5 minutes, just to take the crunch out but not enough to let the cauliflower become soggy.

3. Remove the cauliflower from the skillet and place in a bowl until ready to use. Toss with chopped herbs and additional olive oil for a simple side, top with sautéed veggies and protein, or use in your favorite recipe.

Per Serving: Calories: 92, Total Fat: 9g, Total Carbs: 3g, Net Carbs: 2g, Fiber: 1g, Protein: 1g; Sodium: 595mg

Macros: Fat: 87%, Carbs: 10%, Protein: 3%

Herbed Butter

EGG-FREE, GLUTEN-FREE, NUT-FREE, VEGETARIAN

Makes ½ cup
Prep Time: 10 minutes

½ cup (1 stick) butter, at
　　room temperature
1 garlic clove, finely minced
2 teaspoons finely chopped
　　fresh rosemary
1 teaspoon finely chopped
　　fresh oregano
½ teaspoon salt

This is another great addition to a Ketogenic Mediterranean kitchen. Use along with olive oil to flavor vegetables or grilled fish. Mix a tablespoon of this into scrambled eggs for a true brunch treat or try slathering it on a keto-friendly bread such as the Versatile Sandwich Round (page 169).

1. In a food processor, combine the butter, garlic, rosemary, oregano, and salt and pulse until the mixture is well combined, smooth, and creamy, scraping down the sides as necessary. Alternatively, you can whip the ingredients together with an electric mixer.

2. Using a spatula, scrape the butter mixture into a small bowl or glass container and cover. Store in the refrigerator for up to 1 month.

Per Serving (1 tablespoon): Calories: 103, Total Fat: 12g, Total Carbs: 0g, Net Carbs: 0g, Fiber: 0g, Protein: 0g; Sodium: 227mg

Macros: Fat: 99%, Carbs: 0%, Protein: 1%

Homemade Stock, Two Ways: Fish and Chicken

DAIRY-FREE, EGG-FREE, GLUTEN-FREE, NUT-FREE

Nothing—and I mean absolutely nothing—makes a simple soup or stew pop like homemade stock. I like to make a fish stock with the discarded heads, bones, and tails of fish, as well as shrimp peels. If I've got them on hand, crab or lobster shells are great to throw in for extra flavor. I make chicken stock with the leftovers from a roasted chicken dinner or when I have purchased a store-bought rotisserie chicken in a pinch. It's a beautifully sustainable way to use the entire bird. You can store stock in the freezer in 2-cup servings for convenience.

Fish Stock

Makes 6 cups
Prep Time: 10 minutes
Cook Time: 1 hour

Head and bones of 3 to 4 pounds
   of fish or heads and peels of
   2 to 3 pounds shrimp
1 unpeeled small onion,
   quartered
2 celery stalks, cut into 4 to
   6 pieces
2 garlic cloves, smashed
2 bay leaves
2 teaspoons salt
10 black peppercorns
6 cups water
1 cup dry white wine (optional)

1. In a large stockpot, place the fish parts, onion, celery, garlic, bay leaves, salt, and peppercorns. Add the water and white wine (if using) and bring to a boil.

2. Cover, reduce the heat to low, and simmer for about 45 minutes.

3. Using a slotted spoon or a fine-mesh strainer, strain the stock, discarding all solid pieces. Store in the refrigerator for up to 3 days or in the freezer for up to 3 months.

Per Serving (1 cup): Calories: 40, Total Fat: 2g, Total Carbs: 0g, Net Carbs: 0g, Fiber: 0g, Protein: 5g; Sodium: 775mg

Macros: Fat: 43%, Carbs: 4%, Protein: 53%

Chicken Stock

Makes 8 cups
Prep Time: 10 minutes
Cook Time: 2 hours

1 rotisserie chicken carcass or
    bones from 4 to 6 pounds of
    chicken pieces

1 unpeeled small onion,
    quartered

2 celery stalks, cut into 4 to
    6 pieces

1 cup fresh flat-leaf Italian
    parsley sprigs

2 garlic cloves, smashed

12 sprigs thyme

2 bay leaves

2 teaspoons salt

10 black peppercorns

8 cups water

1. In a large stockpot, place the chicken bones, onion, celery, parsley, garlic, thyme, bay leaves, salt, and peppercorns. Add the water and bring to a boil.

2. Cover, reduce the heat to low, and simmer for about 2 hours.

3. Using a slotted spoon or a fine-mesh strainer, strain the stock, discarding all solid pieces. Store in the refrigerator for up to 3 days or in the freezer for up to 3 months.

Per Serving (1 cup): Calories: 46, Total Fat: 2g, Total Carbs: 4g, Net Carbs: 4g, Fiber: 0g, Protein: 3g; Sodium: 775mg

Macros: Fat: 30%, Carbs: 42%, Protein: 28%

Seedy Crackers

Makes 24 crackers
Prep Time: 25 minutes
Cook Time: 15 minutes

1 cup almond flour
1 tablespoon sesame seeds
1 tablespoon flaxseed
1 tablespoon chia seeds
¼ teaspoon baking soda
¼ teaspoon salt
Freshly ground black pepper
1 large egg, at room
   temperature

These grain-free crackers satisfy a craving for something crunchy without compromising gut healing. Enjoy them topped with smoked salmon or a slice of avocado sprinkled with salt.

1. Preheat the oven to 350°F.

2. In a large bowl, combine the almond flour, sesame seeds, flaxseed, chia seeds, baking soda, salt, and pepper and stir well.

3. In a small bowl, whisk the egg until well beaten. Add to the dry ingredients and stir well to combine and form the dough into a ball.

4. Place one layer of parchment paper on your countertop and place the dough on top. Cover with a second layer of parchment and, using a rolling pin, roll the dough to ⅛-inch thickness, aiming for a rectangular shape.

5. Cut the dough into 1- to 2-inch crackers and bake on parchment until crispy and slightly golden, 10 to 15 minutes, depending on thickness. Alternatively, you can bake the large rolled dough prior to cutting and break into free-form crackers once baked and crispy.

6. Store in an airtight container in the fridge for up to 1 week.

Per Serving (6 crackers): Calories: 119, Total Fat: 9g, Total Carbs: 4g, Net Carbs: 1g, Fiber: 3g, Protein: 5g; Sodium: 242mg

Macros: Fat: 68%, Carbs: 15%, Protein: 17%

References

Altomare, R., Cacciabaudo, F., Damiano, G., et al. "The Mediterranean Diet: A history of health." *Iranian Journal of Public Health*, 42 (5) (2013): 449–457.

Aude, Y. W., Agatston, A. S., Lopez-Jimenez, F., et al. "The National Cholesterol Education Program Diet vs a diet lower in carbohydrates and higher in protein and monounsaturated fat: A randomized trial." *Archives of Internal Medicine*. 64(19) (2004): 2141–2146. doi:10.1001/archinte.164.19.2141.

Campos, H., J. J. Genest, Jr, E. Blijlevens, J. R. McNamara, J. L. Jenner, J. M. Ordovas, P. W. Wilson, and E. J. Schaefer. "Low density lipoprotein particle size and coronary artery disease." *Arteriosclerosis and Thrombosis: A Journal of Vascular Biology*, 12 (1992): 187–195. doi.org/10.1161/01.ATV.12.2.187.

Chianese, R., Coccurello, R., Viggiano, A., Scafuro, M., Fiore, M., Coppola, G., Operto, F. F., Fasano S, Laye S, Pierantoni R, Meccariello R. "Impact of dietary fats on brain functions." *Current Neuropharmacology*, 16(7) (2018):1059-1085. doi: 10.2174/1570159X15666171017102547.

Creighton, Brent C., et al. "Paradox of hypercholesterolaemia in highly trained, keto-adapted athletes." *BMJ Open Sport & Exercise Medicine*, vol. 4,1 e000429 (4 October 2018). doi:10.1136/bmjsem-2018-000429.

Dashti, H. M., Mathew, T. C., Hussein, T., Asfar, S. K., Behbahani, A., Khoursheed, M. A., Al-Sayer, H. M., Bo-Abbas, Y. Y., Al-Zaid, N. S. "Long-term effects of a ketogenic diet in obese patients." *Experimental and Clinical Cardiology*, 9(3) (2004 Fall): 200–5.

Fontana, Luigi, Klein, Samuel, Holloszy, John O., Premachandra, Bhartur N. "Effect of Long-Term Calorie Restriction with Adequate Protein and Micronutrients on Thyroid Hormones." *The Journal of Clinical Endocrinology & Metabolism*, v 91, 8 (1 August 2006): 3232–3235. doi.org/10.1210/jc.2006-0328.

Foster, G. D., Wyatt, H. R., Hill, J. O., McGuckin, B. G., Brill, C., Mohammed, B. S., Szapary, P. O., Rader, D. J., Edman, J. S., and Klein, S. "A randomized trial of a low-carbohydrate diet for obesity." *New England Journal of Medicine*, 348 (21) (May 22, 2003): 2082–90.

Gardner, C. D., Kiazand, A., Alhassan, S., Kim, S., Stafford, R. S., Balise, R. R., Kraemer, H. C., King, A.C. "Comparison of the Atkins, Zone, Ornish, and LEARN diets for change in weight and related risk factors among overweight premenopausal women: The A TO Z Weight Loss Study: A randomized trial." *Journal of American Medical Association*, 7:297(9) (2007): 969–77.

Harvard Health Publishing. "Exercising to Relax." https://www.health.harvard.edu/staying-healthy/exercising-to-relax.

Ivanova, E. A., Myasoedova, V. A., Melnichenko, A. A., Grechko, A. V., & Orekhov, A. N. "Small dense low-density lipoprotein as biomarker for atherosclerotic diseases." *Oxidative Medicine and Cellular Longevity*, 1273042 (2017). doi:10.1155/2017/1273042.

Kosinski, C., Jornayvaz, F. R. "Effects of ketogenic diets on cardiovascular risk factors: evidence from animal and human studies." *Nutrients*. 19:9 (5) (May 2017): pii: E517. doi:10.3390/nu9050517.

Mavropoulos, John C., Yancy, William S., Hepburn, Juanita, and Westman, Eric C. "The effects of a low-carbohydrate, ketogenic diet on the polycystic ovary syndrome: A pilot study." *Nutrition & Metabolism*, 2:35 (2005). doi:10.1186/1743-7075-2-35.

Mayo Clinic. "Chronic stress puts your health at risk." https://www.mayoclinic.org/healthy-lifestyle/stress-management/in-depth/stress/art-20046037.

Mobbs, C. V., Mastaitis, J., Isoda, F., and Poplawski, M. "Treatment of diabetes and diabetic complications with a ketogenic diet." *Journal of Child Neurology*, 28(8) (2013 Aug): 1009–14. doi:10.1177/0883073813487596.

Packard, Chris, FRCPath, Caslake, Muriel, PhD, and Shepherd, James, FRSE. "The role of small, dense low density lipoprotein (LDL): A new look." *International Journal of Cardiology*, v 74, Supplement 1 (30 June 2000): S17-S22. doi.org/10.1016/S0167-5273(99)00107-2.

Samaha, F., M.D., Iqbal, N., et al. "A low-carbohydrate as compared with a low-fat diet in severe obesity." *New England Journal of Medicine*, 348 (2003): 2074-2081. doi:10.1056 /NEJMoa022637.

St-Onge, M.P., Lamarche, B., Mauger, J. F., Jones, P. J. "Consumption of a functional oil rich in phytosterols and medium-chain triglyceride oil improves plasma lipid profiles in men." *Journal of Nutrition*, 133(6) (2003 Jun): 1815–20.

Vidali, S., Aminzadeh, S., Lambert, B., Rutherford, T., Sperl, W., Kofler, B., Feichtinger, R.G. "Mitochondria: The ketogenic diet—A metabolism-based therapy." *International Journal of Biochemistry and Cell Biology*, 63 (2015 Jun): 55-9. doi:10.1016/j.biocel.2015.01.022.

Wood, Richard J., Jeff S. Volek, Yanzhu Liu, Neil S. Shachter, John H. Contois, Maria Luz Fernandez. "Carbohydrate restriction alters lipoprotein metabolism by modifying VLDL, LDL, and HDL subfractiondistribution and size in overweight men." *The Journal of Nutrition*, Volume 136, Issue 2 (February 2006): 384–389, doi.org/10.1093/jn/136.2.384.

World Health Organization. "Fostering healthier and more sustainable diets—learning from the Mediterranean and New Nordic experience." http://www.euro.who.int/en /health-topics/disease-prevention/nutrition/news/news/2018/5/fostering-healthier-and-more-sustainable-diets-learning-from-the-mediterranean-and-new-nordic-experience.

Zinn, C., Wood, M., Williden, M., Chatterton, S., Maunder, E. "Ketogenic diet benefits body composition and well-being but not performance in a pilot case study of New Zealand endurance athletes." *Journal of the International Society of Sports Nutrition*, 12: 14 (22) (2017 Jul). doi:10.1186/s12970-017-0180-0.

Measurement Conversions

	US STANDARD	US STANDARD (OUNCES)	METRIC (APPROXIMATE)
VOLUME EQUIVALENTS (LIQUID)	2 tablespoons	1 fl. oz.	30 mL
	¼ cup	2 fl. oz.	60 mL
	½ cup	4 fl. oz.	120 mL
	1 cup	8 fl. oz.	240 mL
	1½ cups	12 fl. oz.	355 mL
	2 cups or 1 pint	16 fl. oz.	475 mL
	4 cups or 1 quart	32 fl. oz.	1 L
	1 gallon	128 fl. oz.	4 L
VOLUME EQUIVALENTS (DRY)	⅛ teaspoon		0.5 mL
	¼ teaspoon		1 mL
	½ teaspoon		2 mL
	¾ teaspoon		4 mL
	1 teaspoon		5 mL
	1 tablespoon		15 mL
	¼ cup		59 mL
	⅓ cup		79 mL
	½ cup		118 mL
	⅔ cup		156 mL
	¾ cup		177 mL
	1 cup		235 mL
	2 cups or 1 pint		475 mL
	3 cups		700 mL
	4 cups or 1 quart		1 L
	½ gallon		2 L
	1 gallon		4 L
WEIGHT EQUIVALENTS	½ ounce		15 g
	1 ounce		30 g
	2 ounces		60 g
	4 ounces		115 g
	8 ounces		225 g
	12 ounces		340 g
	16 ounces or 1 pound		455 g

	FAHRENHEIT (F)	CELSIUS (C) (APPROXIMATE)
OVEN TEMPERATURES	250°F	120°F
	300°F	150°C
	325°F	180°C
	375°F	190°C
	400°F	200°C
	425°F	220°C
	450°F	230°C

Index

W

Y

Z

Acknowledgments

This project really got its start decades ago when I was inspired by the fresh and robust flavors of Mediterranean cuisine while living in Spain. I so appreciate my time and experience living in that beautiful country and will forever be grateful to my parents for enabling me to do so.

Across the years, all of my foodie friends, neighbors, clients, and family members that love a good meal are the reason I have been able to continue doing what I love to do. I am grateful for you all in my life!

I want to thank my editor, Ada Fung, and her fantastic team at Callisto Media, who provided inspiration for this work and have made all the little details come alive, allowing me to focus on what I do best: healing through nutritious food.

And a big thank-you to my supportive husband and children, who never grow tired of taste-testing and offering candid feedback. Brent, Harper, Luke, and Evan, you inspire me every day and I love you more than words can express.

About the Author

Molly Devine, RD is a registered dietitian who specializes in digestive health, healthy weight management, and chronic disease prevention through integrative and functional nutrition. She is an advocate for sustainable lifestyle change through nutrition intervention and founder of Eat Your Keto, a nutrition counseling and individualized meal-planning service focusing on customized whole foods–based diets for disease prevention and management. She also serves as the director of nutrition for trumacro Nutrition, a medical foods company offering therapeutic ketogenic products, including precooked delivery meals.

Molly is the author of *The Natural Candida Cleanse: A Healthy Treatment Guide to Improve Your Microbiome in Two Weeks*, the coauthor of *The Ketogenic Lifestyle: How to Fuel Your Best,* and a regular contributor to nutrition-based online media outlets, such as *Shape* magazine, *Insider*, *Greatist*, *HuffPost*, *Brides* magazine, and ABC11 *Eyewitness News*.

Molly received her bachelor of science in nutrition sciences from North Carolina Central University and completed her dietetic internship through Meredith College. She also holds a bachelor of science in languages and linguistics from Georgetown University. She lives in Durham, North Carolina, with her family.